MASTERING GIT AND GITHUB FOR VERSION CONTROL

Collaborate and Manage Your Code Like a Pro

THOMPSON CARTER

TABLE OF CONTENTS

Introduction

Mastering Git and GitHub for Developers"

Version control is an essential part of modern software development. It allows developers to track and manage changes in their codebase, collaborate seamlessly with teams, and maintain the integrity and history of their work. **Git**, a distributed version control system, is one of the most widely used tools for this purpose. And when paired with **GitHub**, a web-based platform that facilitates Git repository hosting and collaborative workflows, developers can maximize the power of version control while working in dynamic, ever-evolving environments.

This book, **Mastering Git and GitHub for Developers**, is designed to provide both beginners and experienced developers with the knowledge and skills needed to work effectively with Git and GitHub. Whether you're just starting out or looking to deepen your understanding of advanced version control practices, this book covers a wide range of topics that will enable you to master Git and GitHub in professional development environments.

The Importance of Git and GitHub in Modern Development

Git has become the de facto standard for version control in software development due to its speed, flexibility, and distributed nature. Unlike older version control systems, Git allows every developer to have a full copy of the repository, including its entire history, on their local machine. This decentralization not only makes it faster to work offline, but also improves reliability by reducing the dependency on a central server.

GitHub, a platform built on top of Git, has transformed the way developers collaborate on code. It offers powerful tools for collaboration, such as pull requests, issue tracking, and code reviews, making it easier for teams to contribute, manage, and deploy code in open-source and private projects alike.

This book will guide you through using Git and GitHub to their full potential, providing you with both the theoretical knowledge and practical skills needed to integrate version control and collaborative workflows into your projects.

Who This Book Is For

This book is aimed at developers of all experience levels who want to understand and use Git and GitHub to manage their codebase. Whether you are:

- A **beginner** who has just started learning Git and GitHub and wants to master the basics.
- A **junior developer** seeking to improve your Git workflow for more efficient collaboration with a team.

- An **experienced developer** looking to explore advanced Git features, workflows, and best practices for handling large-scale projects and complex team collaborations.

The book is organized into chapters that gradually build on each other, taking you from fundamental concepts to more advanced techniques. Along the way, you'll encounter real-world examples and practical exercises that will help you apply your knowledge in actual development environments.

What You Will Learn

This book covers a broad spectrum of Git and GitHub concepts and practices that are essential for modern software development:

1. **Git Basics and Setup**: Learn how to set up Git, configure your environment, and understand key concepts like repositories, commits, branches, and remotes.
2. **Advanced Git Features**: Dive deep into advanced Git features like rebasing, merging, stashing, and working with submodules. Master how to resolve conflicts, undo changes, and manage branches effectively.
3. **GitHub for Collaboration**: Explore how to use GitHub for team collaboration, including forking repositories, submitting pull requests, reviewing code, and managing issues. Learn how to set up effective workflows for large teams.

4. **CI/CD and Automation**: Understand how to integrate **Continuous Integration (CI)** and **Continuous Deployment (CD)** into your GitHub workflows using GitHub Actions. Learn how to automate testing, deployments, and more.
5. **Version Control for Open Source**: Discover the process of contributing to open-source projects on GitHub, including how to fork repositories, work with maintainers, and submit pull requests to contribute to the community.
6. **Git Best Practices for Teams**: Learn best practices for working in teams, including strategies for managing large repositories, resolving merge conflicts, and scaling workflows in complex projects.
7. **Troubleshooting Git**: Gain the ability to troubleshoot common Git issues, such as merge conflicts, authentication errors, and failed commits. Learn how to recover from mistakes and keep your workflow smooth.

Real-World Examples and Case Studies

Throughout the book, we provide **real-world examples** that demonstrate how Git and GitHub can be used to solve practical problems encountered by developers in the workplace. Whether it's fixing a mistake in a commit history, resolving a merge conflict in a large team, or managing third-party dependencies through submodules, the case studies will give you the tools to handle complex Git workflows and team collaboration challenges.

One such example is managing a multi-developer project with complex workflows. As your team grows, maintaining a smooth Git workflow becomes more challenging. We will explore how to set up GitHub workflows that scale efficiently in larger teams and handle the intricacies of working with feature branches, releases, and hotfixes.

Why Master Git and GitHub?

Mastering Git and GitHub is crucial for every developer in today's collaborative software development environment. Whether you're working on a solo project, contributing to open-source, or collaborating with a team of developers, Git and GitHub are indispensable tools for version control and code collaboration.

- **Efficiency**: Git allows you to manage your codebase efficiently with powerful tools for branching, merging, and history tracking. GitHub adds a collaborative layer with pull requests, code reviews, and integrated issue tracking, making team workflows more efficient and organized.
- **Collaboration**: GitHub enables seamless collaboration among developers, allowing them to work on different features simultaneously without overwriting each other's work. It's the go-to platform for open-source contributions, where thousands of developers can work together on large projects.

- **Career Advancement**: Understanding Git and GitHub is a fundamental skill for modern software development. Proficiency in these tools will set you apart in the job market, making you a more valuable contributor to any development team.

How to Use This Book

The book is organized into logical sections that follow a clear progression from the basics of Git to more advanced topics. Each chapter builds on the knowledge gained in previous chapters. You can either read the book sequentially or jump to specific chapters that interest you.

1. **Beginner-level chapters** will introduce you to basic Git concepts like setting up your environment, committing changes, branching, and using GitHub for collaboration.
2. **Intermediate-level chapters** will dive into more advanced features such as merge strategies, rebasing, and troubleshooting.
3. **Advanced chapters** will focus on scaling workflows in large teams, CI/CD automation with GitHub Actions, and best practices for contributing to open-source.

Throughout the book, we encourage you to follow along with the examples, try out the commands on your own repositories, and apply the lessons in real-world scenarios.

Mastering Git and GitHub for Developers is your comprehensive guide to becoming a proficient Git user and collaborating effectively using GitHub. Whether you are just starting out or looking to deepen your knowledge of Git and GitHub, this book will provide you with the skills and confidence needed to manage code, contribute to open-source projects, and work seamlessly within teams.

By the end of this book, you'll have a solid understanding of Git's core principles, advanced features, and best practices, making you a more efficient and confident developer ready to tackle any project, from small teams to large-scale enterprise applications.

Happy coding!

Chapter 1: Introduction to Version Control

The Critical Role of Version Control in Modern Software Development

In the rapidly evolving landscape of software development, collaboration, speed, and quality are paramount. Version control plays a critical role in achieving these objectives by providing developers with tools to track, manage, and share their code efficiently.

Why Version Control is Essential

Version control systems (VCS) offer a structured way to record the history of changes to files, enabling developers to work simultaneously on different features, fix bugs without fear of losing their progress, and maintain a clean history of how the codebase has evolved over time. This system is especially important in:

1. **Team Collaboration**: Software development is often a team effort, with multiple developers contributing to a codebase. Without version control, collaboration becomes a logistical nightmare. Version control enables team members to work in parallel, independently making changes to the codebase without affecting each other's work. Git allows users to manage these parallel efforts, providing clear instructions on how to integrate their work with the rest of the team.

2. **Efficiency**: Without version control, the risk of error increases significantly. Developers might inadvertently overwrite each other's work, lose track of their changes, or have difficulty understanding what was changed in the past. Version control systems, like Git, track all changes, allowing developers to revert to any previous state at any time, minimizing mistakes and wasted time.
3. **Traceability and Accountability**: Version control provides transparency about who changed what and when. Every commit (change) is associated with a specific user, a timestamp, and a meaningful message that describes the change. This can help in tracking bugs, ensuring accountability, and making it easier to understand the purpose behind certain code modifications. For instance, if a bug appears after a specific commit, it's possible to trace the problem back to that change, minimizing debugging time.
4. **Code Review and Quality Control**: When multiple people are working on a project, the quality of the code becomes a major concern. Version control allows for structured code review processes. Developers can create pull requests (PRs) on platforms like GitHub, and teammates can review the changes, ensuring the quality of the code before merging it into the main branch. This also helps detect security vulnerabilities, bugs, or logic errors before they are incorporated into the final product.

Version Control and Software Development Lifecycle

In the software development lifecycle (SDLC), version control plays a critical role in both the **development** and **maintenance** phases of the project.

- **Development**: During the development phase, version control allows developers to create branches for specific features or bug fixes. These branches allow developers to work independently on different parts of the project, avoiding conflicts with others' work. When the work is complete, the developer can merge the changes back into the main branch.
- **Maintenance**: Version control is invaluable when it comes to maintaining software after its initial release. Software is rarely perfect on the first try. Developers may need to roll back certain changes, add new features, or fix bugs without disturbing the existing functionality. With version control, it's easy to identify which changes introduced bugs or regressions and roll them back.

What is Git and Why GitHub?

Git: The Power Behind Version Control

Git is a distributed version control system (DVCS), meaning that every developer working on a project has a complete copy of the entire repository, including its history, on their own machine. This contrasts with centralized version control systems, where a single central server stores the repository, and developers check out files from there.

Git's distributed nature offers several advantages:

1. **Speed**: Git is fast. Since it operates locally (i.e., most commands don't require an internet connection), it performs operations like commit, branch, merge, and log much more quickly than centralized systems. Developers can commit their work locally and synchronize with the remote repository at their convenience.
2. **Branching and Merging**: Git allows for advanced branching and merging capabilities. Developers can easily create new branches to experiment with different features or fixes, without affecting the main codebase (often referred to as the "master" or "main" branch). When the work is finished, it can be merged back into the main branch. Git uses an efficient mechanism for merging changes, which ensures that work on different branches can be combined without unnecessary complications.
3. **Offline Capabilities**: Since Git stores the full history of a project on every developer's machine, they can work offline without losing the ability to commit changes, view the history, or switch branches. Once they're back online, they

can push their changes to a central repository like GitHub or GitLab.

4. **Security and Integrity**: Git ensures the integrity of your codebase. Each commit is secured with a cryptographic hash, ensuring that the code hasn't been tampered with. If someone tries to change a commit or alter the history, the hash changes, signaling that something is wrong. This adds an additional layer of security and confidence in the code you're working on.

GitHub: The Collaborative Layer

While Git is the version control system, **GitHub** serves as a platform to host Git repositories and adds a social layer for collaboration. GitHub makes it easier to interact with repositories and integrate Git into a team's workflow.

- **Remote Repositories**: GitHub hosts your Git repositories remotely, allowing developers from anywhere in the world to access and contribute to the project. Instead of pushing changes to a local repository, developers can push to a central repository on GitHub, making collaboration possible across distributed teams.
- **Pull Requests and Code Reviews**: GitHub introduces the concept of pull requests (PRs), which are requests to merge code changes from one branch into another. Pull requests are central to the GitHub collaboration workflow, enabling

teams to review code before it's integrated into the main branch. This is critical for maintaining high code quality, ensuring that all changes are peer-reviewed, and enabling smooth communication between developers.

- **Issue Tracking**: GitHub also offers issue tracking, making it easier to log bugs, feature requests, or discussions about the project. Issues can be tagged, assigned to specific developers, and linked to commits and pull requests, creating a clear record of work.
- **Open Source and Community**: GitHub hosts millions of open-source projects, enabling developers to contribute to public repositories. This has fostered an incredible culture of community-driven development, where developers share their work, collaborate with others, and improve the software ecosystem.

The Problem Without Version Control: Versioning Chaos

Without version control, managing code becomes increasingly difficult, especially as the project grows in complexity and the team size increases. Here are some problems that arise in the absence of version control:

1. **Overwritten Code**: In a team setting, developers are constantly modifying the same files. Without version control,

there's a high likelihood that one developer's changes will overwrite another's, leading to lost work. A developer might accidentally delete an important section of code or unintentionally modify a crucial file. With no history to fall back on, this could lead to the team losing significant progress.

2. **Confusion and Lack of Clarity**: In a versioning-free environment, tracking who made which changes and when becomes impossible. Developers could be working on outdated versions of files without realizing it, causing confusion and a lack of synchronization across the team. Furthermore, this makes troubleshooting and fixing bugs extremely difficult, as there's no way to know the source of a particular bug or issue.
3. **Difficulty in Collaboration**: Without a system to manage changes and communicate those changes with others, developers will likely step on each other's toes. Without clear systems for merging, resolving conflicts, and updating code, collaboration becomes a tedious process of emailing versions of files back and forth. This process doesn't scale well when the team expands or when there are multiple contributors.
4. **No Rollback or Recovery**: In the absence of version control, when things go wrong, there is no easy way to revert changes. Developers might be forced to manually restore old versions

of the code, which is error-prone and time-consuming. Even if the team employs manual backup systems (like copying the project to a new directory every day), it's easy to lose track of changes or accidentally overwrite important files.

5. **Scaling Problems**: As the project grows and more people get involved, the issues become even more pronounced. Manual processes like email-based collaboration, file sharing, and versioning via manual snapshots will break down under the weight of more contributors. What once seemed manageable for a small group of developers becomes a logistical nightmare as the team grows and the codebase becomes more complex.

Real-World Example: A Software Development Team Without Version Control

Let's take a more detailed look at the disastrous consequences a software team might face without version control.

Scenario: A development team of five people is working on a project without version control. They have a shared folder on a server where everyone saves their work. They communicate via email and use spreadsheets to track changes.

1. **Developer A** starts building a new feature but forgets to notify others about the structure of their changes. Developer

B is working on a different feature but ends up modifying the same file as Developer A.

2. **Developer C** encounters a bug and fixes it by changing a crucial function, but they don't communicate it to the rest of the team. Later, Developer D unknowingly reintroduces the same bug in their code, assuming that Developer C's fix was already implemented.
3. **Developer E** adds a new module and creates new files, but due to the lack of versioning, they don't check if the module interferes with the existing work. The module contains errors that aren't noticed until later when the codebase has grown too large to easily troubleshoot.

After weeks of development, the team realizes that many parts of the project are inconsistent. Files have been overwritten, bugs have gone undetected, and there's no clear history to explain why certain decisions were made.

When they attempt to merge the different parts of the code, they realize there's no easy way to reconcile all the changes. Some code is outdated, others are incomplete, and there's no clear version of the codebase to go back to.

The team is forced to spend weeks cleaning up the mess—debugging code, reworking modules, and manually tracking changes. By the time they're done, they've lost a significant amount of productivity.

This example illustrates just how disastrous the absence of version control can be for a software team. Version control, through systems like Git, eliminates these issues by providing clear tracking, collaboration tools, and rollback options.

In the following chapters, we'll dive deeper into how Git and GitHub help solve these problems, making collaboration efficient, reliable, and scalable for modern software teams.

Chapter 2: Understanding Git Basics

Git vs. Other Version Control Systems (SVN, Mercurial)

Git has revolutionized the way software development teams handle version control. However, Git is not the only version control system (VCS) available. Before Git became the industry standard, developers used centralized version control systems (CVCS) like **Subversion (SVN)** and **Mercurial**, and it's important to understand how Git differs from these systems.

Centralized Version Control (SVN)

Subversion (SVN) is one of the most widely used centralized version control systems. In SVN, there is a **central repository** where all the code is stored. Developers retrieve a copy of the code from this central repository, make changes, and then commit those changes back to the central server.

- **Centralized**: SVN has a single central repository. If the central server is down, developers can't access the code or commit new changes.
- **History Tracking**: SVN tracks changes over time, but only the current version of the code is checked out by each developer. This means if a developer wants to go back to a previous version, they need to manually fetch that version from the central server.

- **Branching and Merging**: SVN offers branching and merging capabilities, but they are more cumbersome and less efficient than Git's. SVN's branching can be slow and requires more coordination to merge branches, which can often lead to conflicts.

Git improves upon SVN by being **distributed**, meaning every developer has their own copy of the entire repository with the full history of the project. This allows for faster operations, offline access, and more flexible branching and merging.

Distributed Version Control (Git)

Unlike SVN, Git is **distributed**, meaning each developer's machine holds a full copy of the entire repository. Git tracks not only the latest version of files, but also the history of every change, making it easy to revert to previous versions or experiment with new features.

- **Offline Capability**: Developers can work offline with Git since their full repository is stored locally. All actions like committing, branching, and viewing history can be done without needing access to a central server.
- **Efficiency**: Git's operations (e.g., commit, merge, and rebase) are much faster compared to SVN because Git only needs to access the local repository for most tasks.
- **Branching and Merging**: Git's branching and merging features are far more efficient. Git allows you to create and

switch between branches seamlessly, and it can automatically merge changes when switching between branches or merging contributions from different developers.

Mercurial (Hg)

Mercurial, like Git, is a **distributed version control system**. It is known for being simpler and easier to use than Git, with an easier learning curve. However, Git has become more popular due to its flexibility and extensive feature set.

- **Similarities to Git**: Both Mercurial and Git are distributed systems, meaning developers can work offline, and both allow efficient branching and merging.
- **Differences from Git**: Git has a more extensive ecosystem, with tools like GitHub and GitLab offering robust collaboration features. Mercurial has fewer third-party tools available and does not have the same level of integration with popular CI/CD platforms.

In , Git offers greater flexibility, speed, and efficiency compared to older version control systems like SVN and Mercurial. Its distributed nature and advanced branching/merging capabilities have made it the version control system of choice for modern development.

Key Concepts: Repositories, Commits, Branches, and Remotes

In order to effectively use Git, it's essential to understand some key concepts: **repositories**, **commits**, **branches**, and **remotes**. These are the building blocks of a Git workflow, and they work together to help you manage your project and track changes.

Repositories (Repos)

A **repository** (or **repo**) is where all the files, history, and configurations of a project are stored. There are two types of repositories in Git:

1. **Local Repository**: This is the repository stored on your computer. It contains the entire history of your project and allows you to work offline. Every time you make a commit or create a branch, these changes are stored locally.
2. **Remote Repository**: A remote repository is a copy of your repository that is stored on a server (e.g., GitHub, GitLab, Bitbucket). It serves as a centralized location for sharing your code with others and syncing changes.

Commits

A **commit** in Git is essentially a snapshot of your project at a specific point in time. It records the changes made to the files in your repository and allows you to track the history of those changes. Every commit has the following components:

- **A unique identifier (hash)**: Each commit is given a unique hash (a long string of letters and numbers), which ensures the integrity of the commit and helps differentiate it from other commits.
- **Commit message**: A short description of what changes were made and why. Commit messages should be clear and concise to explain the purpose of the change.
- **Timestamp**: The time when the commit was made.
- **Author**: The person who made the commit.

In Git, each commit is linked to its parent commit(s). This forms a chain of commits, allowing you to review the entire history of your project and even revert to an earlier version if necessary.

Branches

A **branch** in Git is essentially a parallel version of your code. It allows you to work on different tasks or features without affecting the main codebase. Here's how branches work:

- **Master/Main Branch**: The default branch in Git is typically called master or main. This branch usually represents the stable, production-ready version of your project.
- **Feature Branches**: These branches are created to work on specific features or bug fixes. For example, you might create a branch called feature-login to develop a new login system for

your application. This way, your main code remains untouched until the feature is complete.

- **Switching Branches**: One of Git's powerful features is the ability to switch between branches easily. If you're working on a new feature and want to check out the current stable version of the code, you can switch to the main branch without interrupting your work.

Branching allows multiple developers to work independently on different features without worrying about conflicts, and when the feature is complete, it can be merged back into the main branch.

Remotes

A **remote** is a version of your repository that is hosted on a server, such as GitHub, GitLab, or Bitbucket. Remotes allow you to share your work with others and sync changes between different developers.

- **Fetching**: Fetching pulls the latest changes from the remote repository but does not update your working directory. This allows you to see changes made by others without affecting your current work.
- **Pushing**: Pushing sends your local commits to a remote repository. This updates the remote repository with your changes, making them available to other team members.

- **Pulling**: Pulling is a combination of fetching and merging. It retrieves changes from the remote repository and automatically merges them with your local copy.
- **Cloning**: Cloning is the process of copying a remote repository to your local machine. This is typically the first step when you start working on a project hosted on GitHub or another platform.

Real-World Example: A Developer Making Changes to Their Project and Tracking Them with Git

Let's explore how Git can be used in a real-world scenario by following a developer through the process of making changes to their project.

Scenario: Sarah is working on a web application, and she needs to fix a bug in the login page. Here's how she would use Git to manage her work:

1. **Initial Setup**: Sarah clones the repository from GitHub to her local machine:

   bash

   ```
   git clone https://github.com/sarah/web-app.git
   ```

2. **Creating a Branch**: Sarah creates a new branch to work on the login page bug:

   ```css
   git checkout -b fix-login-bug
   ```

   Now she's working on the fix-login-bug branch, which is separate from the main codebase.

3. **Making Changes**: Sarah works on the login page and modifies the login.html file to fix the bug. After making her changes, she checks the status of her files:

   ```lua
   git status
   ```

   Git will show that login.html has been modified.

4. **Staging Changes**: Sarah stages the changes she made to login.html for commit:

   ```csharp
   git add login.html
   ```

5. **Committing Changes**: After staging the changes, Sarah commits them with a message explaining the fix:

   sql

```
git commit -m "Fix login bug: correct input validation"
```

6. **Pushing Changes**: Once Sarah has completed her changes and tested them, she pushes the commit to the remote repository on GitHub:

perl

```
git push origin fix-login-bug
```

7. **Creating a Pull Request**: On GitHub, Sarah opens a pull request to merge her fix-login-bug branch into the main branch. She provides a description of the changes and requests a code review from her team.
8. **Merging the Pull Request**: After her team reviews and approves the pull request, Sarah merges the fix-login-bug branch into main, making the fix available to the entire team.

In this example, Sarah effectively uses Git's basic concepts—branches, commits, and remotes—to track her work and collaborate with her team. By using Git, Sarah avoids overwriting her teammates' work, can easily track the history of her changes, and can merge her fixes into the main project without disrupting the stable codebase.

In this chapter, we've laid the foundation for understanding Git's core concepts: repositories, commits, branches, and remotes. We've also seen how Git differs from other version control systems like SVN and Mercurial. In the next chapter, we'll explore how to set up and configure Git to start tracking and managing your code efficiently.

Chapter 3: Installing and Setting Up Git

Git is an essential tool for managing code, and it is relatively easy to install and configure on different operating systems. In this chapter, we will guide you through the process of installing Git on Windows, macOS, and Linux, as well as configuring it for first-time use. We will also cover a real-world example of configuring Git for your first project, ensuring you are ready to start tracking your code effectively.

Installing Git on Different Operating Systems

1. Installing Git on Windows

To install Git on Windows, follow these steps:

1. **Download Git for Windows**:
   - Visit the official Git website: https://git-scm.com/download/win.
   - The download will automatically start. Choose the appropriate version based on your Windows architecture (32-bit or 64-bit).
2. **Run the Installer**:
   - Once the download is complete, open the .exe file to begin the installation process.

- **Setup Options**: During installation, you will be prompted with various setup options:
    - Choose the default editor for Git (e.g., **Vim**, **Notepad++**, or **Visual Studio Code**). You can change this later if necessary.
    - Select the default PATH environment (use the default option: **Git from the command line and also from 3rd-party software**).
    - Enable **Git Bash Here** and **Git GUI Here** for easy access from the Windows Explorer context menu.
    - Choose **HTTPS** for the transport protocol.
    - Leave the rest of the default options as is unless you have specific needs.

3. **Complete Installation**:
    - After reviewing the settings, click on **Install**. Once the installation is complete, you can launch Git by searching for **Git Bash** in your Start menu or by opening **Git GUI**.
4. **Verify Installation**:
    - To ensure that Git was installed correctly, open Git Bash (a terminal-like window) and type the following command:

css

```
git --version
```

This will display the installed version of Git.

2. Installing Git on macOS

To install Git on macOS, there are two main methods: using **Homebrew** (a package manager for macOS) or downloading directly from the Git website.

1. **Using Homebrew (Recommended Method)**:
   - If you don't have Homebrew installed, you can install it by opening a terminal and typing:

     ```
     bash

     /bin/bash -c "$(curl -fsSL https://raw.githubusercontent.com/Homebrew/install/HEAD/install.sh)"
     ```

   - Once Homebrew is installed, run the following command to install Git:

     ```
     brew install git
     ```

2. **Using the Official Git Installer**:
   - Alternatively, visit https://git-scm.com/download/mac and download the .dmg file.

- Open the .dmg file and follow the installation instructions.
- After installation, open the terminal and check the Git version:

```css
git --version
```

3. Installing Git on Linux

On Linux, the process of installing Git depends on the distribution you are using. The following instructions are for the most common distributions.

1. **Ubuntu/Debian-based Systems**:
   - Open the terminal and update your package index:

   ```sql
   sudo apt update
   ```

   - Install Git using the following command:

   ```
   sudo apt install git
   ```

2. **Fedora/RHEL-based Systems**:
   - Open the terminal and use the following command to install Git:

```
sudo dnf install git
```

3. **Verify Installation**:
   - After installation, check the installed version of Git with:

```css
git --version
```

Configuring Git for First-Time Use

After installing Git, it is important to configure it with your personal information so that your commits are properly identified. The first step in configuring Git is to set your **name** and **email**. These settings will be used to label your commits.

1. Set Your Global Username and Email

1. **Configure Your Name**:
   - In the terminal or Git Bash, run the following command, replacing `Your Name` with your actual name:

```arduino
git config --global user.name "Your Name"
```

2. **Configure Your Email**:
   - Similarly, set your email address:

     arduino

     ```
     git config --global user.email "youremail@example.com"
     ```

     This email address will be associated with your commits.

3. **Verify the Configuration**:
   - You can verify that Git has been configured correctly by running:

     css

     ```
     git config --global --list
     ```

     This will display your Git configuration, including the name and email you've set.

2. Setting Default Text Editor

Git requires a text editor for writing commit messages, editing rebase instructions, and other tasks. The default editor may be **Vim** (if you haven't configured it), but many users prefer editors like **Visual Studio Code** or **Sublime Text**. You can configure the default text editor with the following command:

- To set **Visual Studio Code** as the default editor:

```css
git config --global core.editor "code --wait"
```

- To set **Sublime Text** as the default editor:

```arduino
git config --global core.editor "subl -n -w"
```

Alternatively, you can configure any other text editor that you are comfortable with.

3. Enabling Credential Caching (Optional)

If you don't want to type your GitHub credentials every time you push or pull from a remote repository, you can enable **credential caching**. This stores your credentials for a certain period.

- To enable credential caching for 15 minutes, run:

```arduino
git config --global credential.helper 'cache --timeout=900'
```

For more permanent credential storage, you can use the **Git Credential Manager** or **SSH keys**, which we will discuss later in this book.

Real-World Example: Configuring Git for Your First Project

Let's walk through the process of configuring Git for your first project. Imagine you are working on a simple web application, and you need to start using Git for version control. Here's how you would go about setting up Git for this project:

1. Initialize a Git Repository

1. First, navigate to your project folder in the terminal or Git Bash:

   bash

   ```
   cd path/to/your/project
   ```

2. Initialize a new Git repository:

   csharp

   ```
   git init
   ```

   This command will create a new .git directory in your project folder, which will track all your version control information.

2. Create Your First Commit

1. Add all files to the staging area:

   csharp

   ```
   git add .
   ```

This command stages all files in your project for the first commit. You can also add specific files if you don't want to add everything.

2. Commit your files with a meaningful message:

```sql
git commit -m "Initial commit: set up project structure"
```

This will create your first commit, marking the beginning of the version history for your project.

3. Link Your Local Repository to a Remote Repository (GitHub)

If you are using GitHub to host your project remotely, you can link your local repository to a GitHub repository.

1. Create a new repository on GitHub. Don't initialize it with a README, license, or gitignore (since you already initialized the project locally).
2. Copy the URL of your new repository from GitHub. It will look something like:

```arduino
https://github.com/yourusername/your-project.git
```

3. Link your local repository to the GitHub repository:

csharp

```
git remote add origin https://github.com/yourusername/your-project.git
```

4. Push your first commit to GitHub:

```perl
git push -u origin master
```

Now, your local project is linked to a remote repository on GitHub. You can continue to make changes, commit them locally, and push them to GitHub.

In this chapter, we've covered the installation of Git on different operating systems, as well as how to configure Git for first-time use. We also walked through a real-world example of setting up Git for your first project. By the end of this chapter, you should have a working Git setup that allows you to track your changes, collaborate with others, and keep a clear version history of your projects. In the next chapter, we'll dive into creating your first Git repository and making your first commits.

Chapter 4: Your First Git Repository

In this chapter, we will walk you through the process of creating your first Git repository, and we will cover the basic Git commands needed to manage your project with version control. By the end of this chapter, you will know how to create and track changes in a Git repository, including the foundational commands: **git init**, **git add**, and **git commit**. We will also go through a real-world example of turning a personal project into a Git repository to help solidify your understanding.

Creating a Local Repository

The first step in using Git is to initialize a repository. A repository (or "repo") is where Git stores all your project files and the history of changes made to them. A local repository is a version of the project that exists on your local machine, while a remote repository (like on GitHub) is where the project can be shared with others. In this section, we'll focus on creating a **local repository**.

1. Initialize a Local Git Repository

To create a Git repository for your project, follow these steps:

1. **Navigate to Your Project Folder**:
   - Open the terminal or Git Bash and navigate to the folder where your project is stored. You can use the

cd (change directory) command to go to the appropriate directory:

bash

```
cd path/to/your/project
```

2. **Initialize the Repository**:
   - Once inside your project directory, initialize a Git repository by typing:

     csharp

     ```
     git init
     ```

   - This command will create a new subdirectory called .git in your project folder, which Git will use to store version history and configuration information. It won't affect the files in your project folder; it simply starts tracking your files.
   - After running this command, you'll see something like:

     bash

     ```
     Initialized empty Git repository in /path/to/your/project/.git/
     ```

At this point, you have successfully created a **local Git repository**. The next step is to start adding files and tracking changes.

Basic Git Commands: git init, git add, git commit

Git provides a set of commands that allow you to interact with your repository. In this section, we will focus on three basic commands that will help you manage your project and start tracking changes: **git init**, **git add**, and **git commit**.

1. git init

As mentioned earlier, the **git init** command initializes a new Git repository. It essentially sets up Git tracking for the directory you are in.

When you run git init, Git begins tracking changes to all files in that directory, and it creates a .git folder where all your version control information will be stored. This command is only used once to initialize the repository.

2. git add

The **git add** command is used to add files to the staging area. The staging area is where you prepare your changes before committing them. Files in the staging area are tracked by Git and will be included in the next commit.

You can use **git add** to add individual files or all files in the project.

- **To add a single file**:

csharp

```
git add filename.txt
```

This command stages only the filename.txt file.

- **To add all files in the directory**:

```csharp
git add .
```

The period (.) refers to all files in the current directory and its subdirectories, adding them to the staging area.

It's important to remember that **git add** doesn't commit the changes yet; it just stages them for the commit.

3. git commit

Once your changes are staged, you use the **git commit** command to save those changes in the repository's history.

- **To commit staged changes**:

```sql
git commit -m "Your commit message"
```

The -m flag is followed by a commit message that briefly describes the changes you've made. A good commit message is clear and concise, explaining what changes were made and why.

Example commit message:

```sql
git commit -m "Add homepage layout files"
```

After you run the commit command, Git will store the changes in the repository's history, along with the commit message, timestamp, and author information.

Real-World Example: A Personal Project Becoming a Git Repository

Let's walk through an example where you turn your personal project into a Git repository. Suppose you've been working on a small **website project** for a while, and now you want to start using Git to track your progress.

Step 1: Create a Folder for the Project

You have a folder on your computer with the following structure for your website:

```bash
/website-project
   /index.html
   /style.css
   /app.js
```

You want to initialize a Git repository to start tracking changes to the project.

1. **Navigate to the Project Folder**: Open Git Bash or your terminal and change into the project directory:

   bash

   cd /path/to/website-project

2. **Initialize the Git Repository**: Initialize the repository with:

   csharp

   git init

   This will create a .git directory inside the website-project folder, allowing Git to start tracking changes.

Step 2: Add Files to the Repository

Now that you have initialized the Git repository, you need to tell Git which files to track. Let's add all the files in the project directory.

1. **Stage All Files**:

   csharp

   git add .

   This command stages all the files in the project directory (i.e., index.html, style.css, app.js), preparing them for the first commit.

Step 3: Make Your First Commit

Now it's time to commit the changes. Since this is the first time you are committing, you'll include a message like "Initial commit" to mark the start of your project.

1. **Commit the Files**:

   sql

   ```
   git commit -m "Initial commit: Add homepage files"
   ```

   This command saves the changes to the Git history, with the message explaining that you've added the homepage files for your website.

Step 4: Check the Status of Your Repository

At any point, you can check the status of your repository to see which files are staged or modified but not yet committed. Run the following command:

lua

```
git status
```

This will display the current state of the repository, showing you which files are staged, untracked, or modified.

Step 5: View the Commit History

You can view the commit history using the following command:

bash

git log

This will show the list of commits in reverse chronological order, starting with your most recent commit. Since you only have one commit, it will show something like this:

sql

```
commit 9a1b2c3d4e5f6g7h8i9j0k (HEAD -> master)
Author: Your Name <youremail@example.com>
Date:   Mon Apr 26 14:00:00 2024 -0700

    Initial commit: Add homepage files
```

Now, your project is a full-fledged Git repository, and all changes to the files in the project will be tracked by Git.

In this chapter, you learned how to:

- **Create a local Git repository** using git init.
- **Stage files** for commit using git add.
- **Commit changes** to the repository using git commit.
- **Track your project** with basic Git commands.

We also walked through a real-world example of turning a personal website project into a Git repository, tracking changes to the files, and making the first commit. With these basic Git commands under your belt, you can now manage your projects effectively and start building a version history. In the next chapter, we'll explore how to collaborate with others by using **remotes** and **push/pull** operations.

Chapter 5: Committing Changes

In this chapter, we will delve into one of the most important aspects of using Git: committing changes. The commit process is how you save and document the progress of your project. It's the foundation of tracking changes in your codebase, ensuring that you can review, collaborate, and roll back to previous states as needed. We'll also cover best practices for writing commit messages and walk through a real-world example of a web developer's commit cycle.

Making Your First Commit

After initializing your Git repository and staging your files (with git add), the next step is to commit those changes. A **commit** is a snapshot of your repository at a specific point in time. It stores the changes you've made and allows you to record important milestones in your project's development.

1. Basic Commit Command

Once you've added the necessary files to the staging area using the git add command, you can create your first commit with:

sql

```
git commit -m "Your commit message"
```

The -m flag is used to specify the commit message directly in the command line.

For example, after adding files to your project, you can commit them as follows:

sql

```
git commit -m "Initial commit: Set up project structure with index, CSS, and JS files"
```

In this case, you're committing the initial setup of your project, including the core files such as index.html, style.css, and app.js.

2. Staging and Committing Changes Separately

If you make changes to files after your initial commit, Git will not automatically include those changes in the previous commit. Instead, you need to repeat the process of staging and committing.

1. **Stage new changes**: After modifying your project files, use git add to stage the changes.

   csharp

   ```
   git add modified-file.html
   ```

2. **Commit the changes**: Once you've staged the changes, commit them to record the updates.

   sql

   ```
   git commit -m "Fix bug in user login form"
   ```

3. The Commit Process Overview

To summarize the commit process:

- **git add**: This stages changes and tells Git which files to include in the next commit.
- **git commit**: This records the changes into the project history and provides a snapshot of your code at that point in time.
- **Commit Hash**: Every commit is associated with a unique identifier called a **hash**, which is a long string of characters that Git generates automatically. This ensures the integrity of your commit history.

Understanding the Commit Message Structure

A commit message serves two key purposes: it describes the changes that have been made and provides context for why those changes were made. A well-written commit message improves collaboration, makes it easier to understand the project's history, and allows you to review changes quickly in the future.

1. Commit Message Best Practices

A good commit message should be clear, concise, and structured. Here's the common format for commit messages:

- **Title (short)**: The first line should be a brief (around 50 characters) that explains the changes. It should be written in the **imperative mood**, as if you're telling the system what to do. For example:

sql

```
Add new user login feature
```

- **Body (optional, but useful)**: After a blank line, you can provide a more detailed explanation of the changes, why they were necessary, and any important context. The body of the commit message should be wrapped at 72 characters for readability. For example:

vbnet

```
Add new user login feature

This commit adds a new login form to the homepage, allowing users to
authenticate using their username and password. The form was styled to
match the site's theme, and basic validation has been implemented.
```

2. Why Structure Matters

A structured commit message is essential for a few reasons:

- **Clarity**: A well-written message makes it easier for others (or yourself) to understand the intent behind a commit.
- **Tracking**: It helps when you need to revisit your commit history. For example, if you are debugging an issue or

looking for a feature, you can search commit messages to find exactly what you're looking for.

- **Collaboration**: If you're working in a team, clear commit messages reduce confusion and ensure everyone understands the changes.

Real-World Example: A Web Developer's Commit Cycle

Let's walk through a typical commit cycle that a web developer might go through while working on a feature for a website. This will help illustrate how commits work in the context of a larger development workflow.

Scenario: Building a Contact Form

Suppose you are a web developer working on a new feature for a website: a **contact form** where users can submit their name, email, and message. You'll be following the typical process of creating new files, making updates, and committing changes as you go.

Step 1: Set Up the Basic HTML for the Contact Form

1. **Create a new HTML file** for the contact form.

   bash

   ```
   touch contact.html
   ```

2. **Add basic HTML structure** for the form.

html

```
<html>
<head>
  <title>Contact Us</title>
</head>
<body>
  <form action="submit-form.php" method="POST">
    <label for="name">Name:</label>
    <input type="text" id="name" name="name" required><br><br>

    <label for="email">Email:</label>
    <input type="email" id="email" name="email" required><br><br>

    <label for="message">Message:</label><br>
    <textarea id="message" name="message" rows="4" required></textarea><br><br>

    <button type="submit">Submit</button>
  </form>
</body>
</html>
```

3. **Stage and commit the new file** to Git:

sql

```
git add contact.html
git commit -m "Add contact form HTML structure"
```

At this point, you've added a new HTML file and committed the changes with a message explaining that you've set up the contact form's basic structure.

Step 2: Add Styling to the Form

Next, you decide to style the form to make it more user-friendly and visually appealing. You create a new style.css file.

1. **Create the style.css file**:

   bash

   ```
   touch style.css
   ```

2. **Add CSS rules** to style the form:

   css

   ```
   body {
     font-family: Arial, sans-serif;
   }

   form {
     max-width: 600px;
     margin: 0 auto;
   }

   label {
     display: block;
     margin: 10px 0 5px;
   ```

```
}

input, textarea {
  width: 100%;
  padding: 8px;
  margin: 5px 0;
}

button {
  padding: 10px 20px;
  background-color: #4CAF50;
  color: white;
  border: none;
  cursor: pointer;
}

button:hover {
  background-color: #45a049;
}
```

3. **Stage and commit the changes**:

sql

```
git add style.css
git commit -m "Add CSS styles for contact form"
```

Step 3: Implement Form Validation with JavaScript

Now, you want to add some **JavaScript validation** to ensure that the user has filled in all required fields correctly before submitting the form.

1. **Create a script.js file**:

   bash

   ```
   touch script.js
   ```

2. **Write JavaScript to validate the form**:

   javascript

   ```
   document.querySelector("form").addEventListener("submit",
   function(event) {
     var name = document.getElementById("name").value;
     var email = document.getElementById("email").value;
     var message = document.getElementById("message").value;

     if (!name || !email || !message) {
       alert("Please fill in all fields.");
       event.preventDefault();
     }
   });
   ```

3. **Stage and commit the new file**:

   sql

```
git add script.js
git commit -m "Add form validation using JavaScript"
```

Step 4: Test the Feature and Make Final Adjustments

You test the contact form locally, but you realize that the styling for the button is a bit off. You update the CSS to fix the issue.

1. **Modify the CSS** to adjust the button's style.
2. **Stage and commit** the final changes:

   sql

   ```
   git add style.css
   git commit -m "Fix button styling on contact form"
   ```

Step 5: Push Changes to the Remote Repository

Finally, after completing the feature, you push all of your commits to your remote repository on GitHub:

perl

```
git push origin master
```

This makes the changes accessible to others (or yourself) from any machine, and the feature is now part of the project's history.

In this chapter, we learned the importance of **committing changes** in Git. We discussed:

- How to make your first commit using git commit -m.
- Best practices for writing **clear commit messages** that describe the changes made and the reason for those changes.
- A real-world example where a web developer builds a contact form, styles it with CSS, and validates it with JavaScript, committing each significant change along the way.

By following this workflow, you ensure that your project's history remains clean, organized, and easy to navigate. In the next chapter, we will explore **branching** and how to manage different versions of your project using Git.

Chapter 6: Understanding Branches

In this chapter, we will explore one of the most powerful features of Git: **branches**. Branching allows developers to work on new features, bug fixes, or experiments without affecting the main codebase. It is crucial for efficient collaboration and maintaining clean, organized code in software projects. We will discuss what branches are, why they are important, how to create and switch between branches, and conclude with a real-world example of using branches to work on a new app feature.

What Are Branches and Why They Are Important?

A **branch** in Git is essentially a parallel version of your codebase. It allows you to isolate your changes from the main project. This isolation is beneficial because it enables multiple developers to work on different features or bug fixes simultaneously without interfering with each other's work.

Why Branches Are Important:

1. **Parallel Development**: With branches, developers can work on new features or fixes without disrupting the main or stable version of the project. For example, one developer could be working on a new user authentication system in one branch, while another is fixing bugs in a different branch.

2. **Feature Isolation**: Working on separate branches helps keep each feature independent. Once the feature is complete and tested, it can be merged into the main codebase. This isolation prevents incomplete or untested features from affecting the stable version of the project.
3. **Collaboration**: In a team environment, branches allow team members to collaborate efficiently without stepping on each other's toes. Each developer can create a branch for their specific task (e.g., a bug fix or feature development), and when ready, submit their changes to be merged into the main branch.
4. **Version Control**: Branching helps keep the history of changes clean. If a feature is not ready or doesn't work out, it can be discarded without affecting the main codebase, which is invaluable in production environments.

Common Types of Branches:

- **Main (or Master) Branch**: The main branch (formerly called master in Git) is the primary branch where the stable, production-ready version of your code resides.
- **Feature Branch**: A feature branch is created when working on a new feature or enhancement. It allows you to work on the feature in isolation from the main codebase.

- **Bugfix Branch**: Similar to feature branches, bugfix branches are used specifically for addressing issues or bugs within the codebase.
- **Release Branch**: Release branches are created when preparing for a new release. This branch contains final tweaks and bug fixes for the upcoming release.
- **Hotfix Branch**: Hotfix branches are used to make quick fixes in the production codebase. They allow you to fix issues that need immediate attention without waiting for the next release cycle.

Creating, Listing, and Switching Branches

Now that we understand the importance of branches, let's take a look at how to create, list, and switch between branches in Git.

1. Creating a Branch

To create a new branch, use the git branch command followed by the name of the branch. For example, to create a new branch called feature-login, you would run:

```
git branch feature-login
```

This will create the branch, but you'll still be on your current branch (usually main or master).

2. Switching Between Branches

To switch to a newly created branch, use the git checkout command followed by the branch name:

```
git checkout feature-login
```

Alternatively, in newer versions of Git, you can create and switch to a branch in one step using the -b flag:

```css
git checkout -b feature-login
```

This command does two things:

- It creates the feature-login branch.
- It immediately switches to that branch.

3. Listing Branches

To see a list of all the branches in your project, use the following command:

```
git branch
```

The active branch (the one you're currently on) will be marked with an asterisk (*). For example:

```css
* main
  feature-login
  bugfix-header
```

4. Deleting a Branch

Once a branch is no longer needed (for example, after the feature has been merged), you can delete it using the following command:

```
git branch -d feature-login
```

If the branch hasn't been merged yet, Git will prevent you from deleting it unless you force the deletion with:

```
mathematica

git branch -D feature-login
```

Real-World Example: Working on a Feature Branch for a New App Feature

Let's walk through a real-world scenario where you're a developer working on a new feature for a web app. In this example, you will work on a **login feature** and follow the proper Git workflow using branches.

Step 1: Create the Feature Branch

Imagine you've been tasked with adding a new user login feature to an existing app. To start, you would first create a new branch for the feature. This will allow you to work on the feature without affecting the main codebase.

1. **Create and switch to a new feature branch**:

```css
git checkout -b feature-login
```

This creates a branch called feature-login and switches to it immediately. Now you are isolated in this new branch and can begin working on your login functionality.

Step 2: Develop the Feature

Now, you can start working on the feature in your branch. In our example, you might create a new HTML form, write the JavaScript for validation, and set up the backend logic.

For example, you might add a file called login.html with the following content:

```html
<!DOCTYPE html>
<html lang="en">
<head>
   <meta charset="UTF-8">
   <meta name="viewport" content="width=device-width, initial-scale=1.0">
   <title>Login</title>
</head>
<body>
   <form id="loginForm">
      <label for="username">Username:</label>
      <input type="text" id="username" name="username" required><br><br>
      <label for="password">Password:</label>
```

```
    <input type="password" id="password" name="password" required><br><br>
    <button type="submit">Login</button>
  </form>
</body>
</html>
```

After making changes to the code, you would stage and commit your changes:

sql

```
git add login.html
git commit -m "Add login form for user authentication"
```

Step 3: Keep the Feature Branch Up to Date

While you are working on the feature, other developers might be pushing updates to the main branch. To keep your feature branch up to date with the latest changes from main, you need to **merge** those changes into your feature branch.

1. First, switch to the main branch:

   css

   ```
   git checkout main
   ```

2. Fetch the latest changes from the remote repository:

   css

```
git pull origin main
```

3. Switch back to your feature branch:

```
git checkout feature-login
```

4. Merge the changes from main into your feature branch:

```css
git merge main
```

This will ensure your branch is up to date with the latest changes.

Step 4: Testing and Finalizing the Feature

Once the feature is complete and fully tested, you're ready to merge your changes back into the main branch.

1. **Switch to the main branch**:

```css
git checkout main
```

2. **Merge the feature branch into main**:

```sql
git merge feature-login
```

3. After successfully merging, you can delete the feature-login branch since it's no longer needed:

```
git branch -d feature-login
```

4. Finally, push your changes to the remote repository:

```css
git push origin main
```

In this chapter, we've learned about **branches** in Git, including their importance and how they help manage different versions of a project. We also covered:

- **How to create, switch, and list branches** using Git commands like git branch, git checkout, and git checkout -b.
- The process of working on a new **feature branch**, including how to develop a new feature, keep your branch up to date with the latest changes, and merge your feature back into the main branch.
- The importance of using branches to collaborate, test, and ensure your codebase remains clean and stable.

In the next chapter, we will explore how to **merge branches** and handle conflicts that can arise when combining changes from different branches.

Chapter 7: Merging and Resolving Conflicts

In this chapter, we will explore the **merge process** in Git, how it works, and how to resolve merge conflicts effectively. We'll also look at a real-world example where two developers work on the same file, creating a merge conflict, and see how to resolve it in a collaborative environment.

Understanding the Merge Process

Merging is a fundamental part of working with branches in Git. It is the process of combining the changes made in two different branches into a single unified branch. In most workflows, you create a branch to work on a specific feature, bug fix, or improvement. Once the work is complete, you merge the branch back into the main branch (usually main or master).

1. What Happens During a Merge?

When you perform a merge, Git attempts to combine the changes from both branches. If the changes in the branches do not conflict (i.e., the changes are made in different parts of the files), Git will automatically combine them into a new commit. The result is a single commit in the history that contains changes from both branches.

For example:

- **Branch A** has changes to file1.txt and file2.txt.
- **Branch B** has changes to file3.txt.

When you merge Branch B into Branch A, Git will simply apply the changes from file3.txt and combine the changes from file1.txt and file2.txt without any issues.

2. Fast-Forward Merges

In some cases, Git can perform a **fast-forward merge**. This happens when the current branch has no new commits since the branch being merged. In such cases, Git simply moves the pointer of the current branch forward to the commit of the branch being merged. There are no new merge commits because there are no conflicting changes.

Example:

- main branch has only one commit.
- feature-branch has one commit.
- Merging feature-branch into main is a fast-forward merge, and the commit history is linear.

3. Non-Fast-Forward Merges

When both branches have commits that are not shared between them, Git performs a **non-fast-forward merge**, which results in a new merge commit. This commit has two parent commits: one from the current branch and one from the branch being merged. Git will try to automatically combine the changes, but sometimes it will encounter conflicts.

How to Handle Merge Conflicts Effectively

A **merge conflict** occurs when Git is unable to automatically merge changes because the changes made in the two branches are in the same part of the code. For example, two developers might modify the same line in the same file, leading to a conflict that Git cannot resolve without human intervention.

1. Detecting a Merge Conflict

You will see a merge conflict when you attempt to merge two branches. For example, let's say you are on the main branch, and you want to merge the feature-login branch into it.

1. Switch to the main branch:

   css

   ```
   git checkout main
   ```

2. Attempt to merge the feature-login branch:

   sql

   ```
   git merge feature-login
   ```

If there is a conflict, Git will display a message like:

```sql

Automatic merge failed; fix conflicts and then commit the result.
```

At this point, Git will mark the conflicted files and allow you to resolve them manually.

2. Resolving the Conflict

To resolve the conflict, follow these steps:

1. **Identify Conflicted Files**: Git will mark conflicted files with a <<<<<<<, =======, and >>>>>>> section. These markers indicate where the conflict occurred.

   Example:

   ```javascript

   function loginUser(username, password) {
     if (username === "admin" && password === "password123") {
       console.log("Login successful");
     } else {
       console.log("Invalid credentials");
     }
   }
   <<<<<<< HEAD
   function loginUser(username, password) {
     if (username === "admin" && password === "admin123") {
       console.log("Admin login successful");
     } else {
       console.log("Incorrect credentials");
   ```

```
    }
}
=======
function loginUser(username, password) {
    if (username === "admin" && password === "password123") {
        console.log("Login successful");
    } else {
        console.log("Invalid credentials");
    }
}
>>>>>>> feature-login
```

In this example, the code for the loginUser function is different in both branches. The HEAD section is your current branch (main), and the feature-login section contains the changes from the branch being merged.

2. **Resolve the Conflict**: You need to decide how to combine the changes. This could involve choosing one version of the code, combining the changes manually, or rewriting the logic entirely. After editing the file, remove the conflict markers (<<<<<<<, =======, and >>>>>>>).

For example, you might decide to merge the logic from both versions:

javascript

```
function loginUser(username, password) {
    if (username === "admin" && password === "admin123") {
```

```
        console.log("Admin login successful");
    } else if (username === "admin" && password === "password123")
{
        console.log("Login successful");
    } else {
        console.log("Invalid credentials");
    }
}
```

3. **Stage the Resolved Files**: After resolving the conflicts, stage the changes for commit:

```
csharp

git add login.js
```

4. **Commit the Merge**: Once all conflicts are resolved, commit the changes to complete the merge:

```
sql

git commit -m "Resolve merge conflict in loginUser function"
```

This commit will record the resolution of the conflict.

3. Using a Merge Tool

If the conflicts are complex, you can use a **merge tool** to help resolve them. Many Git GUIs and IDEs (e.g., GitKraken, Sourcetree, or Visual Studio Code) come with built-in merge tools that provide a graphical interface to resolve conflicts more easily.

To use a merge tool with Git, run:

```
git mergetool
```

This will open the configured merge tool and allow you to resolve conflicts visually.

Real-World Example: Two Developers Working on the Same File

Let's consider a real-world scenario where two developers, **Alice** and **Bob**, are working on the same file, login.js, which leads to a merge conflict.

Step 1: Alice's Changes

1. Alice is working on the main branch. She adds a simple login form to login.js:

   javascript

   ```javascript
   function loginUser(username, password) {
     if (username === "admin" && password === "admin123") {
       console.log("Admin login successful");
     } else {
       console.log("Invalid credentials");
     }
   }
   ```

2. Alice commits her changes:

```sql
git add login.js
git commit -m "Add login functionality for admin"
```

Step 2: Bob's Changes

1. Bob, who is also working on the feature-login branch, modifies the loginUser function to add more detailed validation:

```javascript
function loginUser(username, password) {
  if (username === "admin" && password === "password123") {
    console.log("Login successful");
  } else {
    console.log("Invalid credentials");
  }
}
```

2. Bob commits his changes:

```sql
git add login.js
git commit -m "Update login validation logic"
```

Step 3: Merging Alice and Bob's Changes

When Alice tries to merge the feature-login branch (which contains Bob's changes) into the main branch, a conflict arises because both Alice and Bob modified the same lines of code in the login.js file.

1. Alice runs the merge command:

   sql

   ```
   git merge feature-login
   ```

2. Git reports a merge conflict.

Step 4: Resolving the Conflict

1. Alice opens login.js and sees the conflict markers indicating the conflicting changes.
2. Alice decides to combine the best parts of both versions, resulting in the following code:

   javascript

   ```
   function loginUser(username, password) {
     if (username === "admin" && password === "admin123") {
       console.log("Admin login successful");
     } else if (username === "admin" && password === "password123")
   {
       console.log("Login successful");
     } else {
       console.log("Invalid credentials");
   ```

```
    }
}
```

3. Alice stages the changes:

```csharp
git add login.js
```

4. Alice commits the resolution:

```sql
git commit -m "Resolve merge conflict in loginUser function"
```

In this chapter, we learned about **merging** in Git and how to handle **merge conflicts**. We covered:

- **What happens during a merge**, including fast-forward and non-fast-forward merges.
- **How to handle merge conflicts**, including using Git conflict markers and resolving the conflict manually or with a merge tool.
- A **real-world example** of two developers working on the same file, leading to a merge conflict, and how to resolve it.

By understanding the merge process and conflict resolution, you can ensure smooth collaboration and maintain a clean and organized codebase. In the next chapter, we will explore **advanced merging techniques**, such as **rebasing** and **cherry-picking**, to help you fine-tune your Git workflow.

Chapter 8: Working with Remote Repositories

In this chapter, we will discuss how to work with **remote repositories** in Git, how to set up and connect a remote repository on GitHub, and walk through a real-world example of pushing your local Git repository to GitHub. This chapter will help you understand the importance of remote repositories, how they enable collaboration, and how you can leverage GitHub to share and manage your projects.

What is a Remote Repository?

A **remote repository** is a version of your Git repository that is hosted on a server, allowing you to access and share your project with others. It acts as a centralized location where the repository can be stored, and multiple developers can push and pull changes to collaborate.

Unlike a **local repository**, which is stored on your own machine, a **remote repository** allows you to keep your work synchronized with others and enables collaboration through features like pull requests, issue tracking, and continuous integration.

Common platforms that host remote repositories include:

- **GitHub**: The most popular Git hosting platform, especially for open-source projects.
- **GitLab**: A platform for managing repositories, CI/CD pipelines, and DevOps tools.
- **Bitbucket**: A platform for Git-based source code hosting, often used for private repositories.

Why Use Remote Repositories?

- **Collaboration**: Remote repositories enable multiple developers to work on the same project by allowing them to push their local changes to a central repository and pull in changes made by others.
- **Backup and Sync**: Remote repositories provide a backup of your code, protecting it from data loss due to local machine failure. They also help sync your code across different machines (e.g., between your work and home computers).
- **Open Source and Sharing**: Remote repositories like those hosted on GitHub allow you to share your project with the public or with a team. You can contribute to open-source projects, submit pull requests, and manage issues.

Setting Up and Connecting a Remote GitHub Repository

GitHub is the most widely used platform for hosting Git repositories, and it integrates seamlessly with Git. Here's how to set up and connect a remote GitHub repository to your local Git repository.

1. Creating a Remote GitHub Repository

1. **Create a GitHub account** (if you don't have one) at https://github.com.
2. **Create a new repository**:
   - Log in to your GitHub account.
   - Click the green **New** button on the repository page or go to https://github.com/new.
   - Fill out the repository name (e.g., my-first-project), description (optional), and choose the repository visibility (public or private).
   - **Do not** initialize the repository with a README, license, or .gitignore if you already have an existing local Git repository. GitHub will provide instructions for pushing your existing project later.
3. **Create the repository** by clicking the **Create repository** button.

At this point, you have a remote repository on GitHub, but you still need to link it to your local repository.

2. Connecting Your Local Repository to the Remote Repository

To link your local Git repository to the newly created remote repository on GitHub, follow these steps:

1. **Copy the remote repository URL**:
   - After creating the repository on GitHub, you'll see the repository's URL at the top of the page. It will look something like:

     perl

     ```
     https://github.com/yourusername/my-first-project.git
     ```

2. **Add the remote repository to your local Git repository**:
   - In your terminal, navigate to your local project directory and run the following command to add the remote repository:

     csharp

     ```
     git remote add origin https://github.com/yourusername/my-first-project.git
     ```

   - The origin keyword refers to the default name for your remote repository. You can change the name of the remote, but origin is the standard.
3. **Verify the connection**:
   - To confirm that the remote repository has been added successfully, use the following command:

```
git remote -v
```

This will list the remote repositories linked to your local project:

```perl
origin https://github.com/yourusername/my-first-project.git (fetch)
origin https://github.com/yourusername/my-first-project.git (push)
```

Real-World Example: Pushing Your Local Repository to GitHub

Let's walk through an example where you have a local repository, and you want to push it to GitHub to make it available remotely.

Step 1: Initialize Your Local Git Repository

Let's assume you've been working on a project locally, and you want to upload it to GitHub.

1. Open your terminal and navigate to your project folder:

   ```bash
   cd /path/to/your/project
   ```

2. Initialize the Git repository (if you haven't already):

```csharp
git init
```

3. Add your project files to the staging area:

```csharp
git add .
```

4. Commit the files to your local repository:

```sql
git commit -m "Initial commit"
```

Step 2: Add the Remote Repository

Now that you've committed your local changes, you need to link your local repository to the remote GitHub repository.

1. Copy the remote repository URL from GitHub.
2. Add the remote repository to your local Git configuration:

```csharp
git remote add origin https://github.com/yourusername/my-first-project.git
```

Step 3: Push Your Local Repository to GitHub

After adding the remote repository, the next step is to push your changes to GitHub.

1. Push your local repository to GitHub:

   ```perl
   git push -u origin master
   ```

   - The `-u` flag sets the upstream reference, meaning the local `master` branch will be connected to the `master` branch on GitHub. The first time you push, you may need to authenticate with your GitHub credentials.

2. Git will now upload your local repository to GitHub. You will see output like this:

   ```bash
   Counting objects: 15, done.
   Delta compression using up to 4 threads.
   Compressing objects: 100% (12/12), done.
   Writing objects: 100% (15/15), 2.05 KiB | 2.05 MiB/s, done.
   Total 15 (delta 0), reused 0 (delta 0)
   To https://github.com/yourusername/my-first-project.git
    * [new branch]      master -> master
   ```

Step 4: Verify the Push

To verify that your files have been pushed to GitHub, navigate to your repository on GitHub in your web browser. You should see your project files in the repository.

Common Commands for Working with Remote Repositories

Here are some of the most common Git commands used when working with remote repositories:

1. **Fetching Changes**: To fetch the latest changes from the remote repository without merging them into your local branch:

   sql

   ```
   git fetch origin
   ```

2. **Pulling Changes**: To fetch and merge the latest changes from the remote repository into your local branch:

   ```
   git pull origin master
   ```

3. **Pushing Changes**: To push your local commits to the remote repository:

   perl

```
git push origin master
```

4. **Listing Remote Repositories**: To list all remote repositories connected to your local repository:

```
git remote -v
```

5. **Removing a Remote**: If you need to remove a remote repository:

```
arduino

git remote remove origin
```

In this chapter, we covered the following topics related to **working with remote repositories** in Git:

- **What remote repositories are** and why they are essential for collaboration and backup.
- **How to set up a remote repository on GitHub** and connect it to your local Git repository.
- A **real-world example** of pushing a local Git repository to GitHub to make it available remotely.
- Common **Git commands** for interacting with remote repositories, including git push, git pull, and git fetch.

Now that you understand how to connect to and work with remote repositories, you are ready to collaborate with others and ensure that your code is safely stored and easily accessible. In the next chapter, we will explore advanced Git workflows, such as using **branches and pull requests** for efficient collaboration.

Chapter 9: Cloning and Forking Repositories

In this chapter, we will discuss two essential Git operations: **cloning** and **forking**. Both operations are used to copy repositories, but they serve different purposes and are used in different workflows. We will cover the **difference between cloning and forking**, how to clone a repository and start working, and provide a **real-world example of contributing to an open-source project by forking**.

Difference Between Cloning and Forking

While **cloning** and **forking** both involve copying a Git repository, they are used in different contexts and serve different purposes:

Cloning

- **What it is**: Cloning is the process of creating a local copy of a remote repository. When you clone a repository, you get a full copy of the project's history, branches, and files on your local machine. This is typically used when you want to start working on a project locally and sync your changes with a remote repository.
- **Where it's used**: Cloning is commonly used when you are contributing to a repository with write access or when you want to download a copy of a repository for personal use.

- **How it works**: When you clone a repository, you get a connection to the original remote repository, and you can pull updates from it or push changes if you have write access.

Forking

- **What it is**: Forking is the process of creating a **copy** of a repository under your own GitHub account. This is commonly done when you want to contribute to someone else's repository without directly modifying the original repository. When you fork a repository, the original repository remains unchanged, and you can make any modifications in your fork.
- **Where it's used**: Forking is most commonly used in open-source projects. You fork a project to propose changes, and once you're done, you can create a pull request to merge your changes back into the original repository.
- **How it works**: After forking a repository, you get a full copy of it under your own GitHub account. You can make changes in this fork without affecting the original repository. If you want to share your changes, you can create a pull request to the original repository, asking the project maintainers to merge your changes.

How to Clone a Repository and Start Working

Cloning a repository is straightforward. It allows you to download a copy of a remote repository to your local machine, where you can start working on it.

Steps to Clone a Repository

1. **Find the Repository on GitHub**:
   - Navigate to the GitHub page of the repository you want to clone. For example, let's say you want to clone a project called awesome-project.
2. **Copy the Repository URL**:
   - On the GitHub repository page, click the **Code** button (usually green) and copy the URL of the repository. It will look something like:

     arduino

     ```
     https://github.com/username/awesome-project.git
     ```
3. **Clone the Repository**:
   - Open your terminal (or Git Bash) and navigate to the directory where you want to store the cloned project.
   - Run the following command:

     bash

     ```
     git clone https://github.com/username/awesome-project.git
     ```

   - This will download the repository and create a new folder named awesome-project containing the entire repository.
4. **Navigate to the Cloned Repository**:
   - After cloning, navigate into the project directory:

```bash
cd awesome-project
```

5. **Start Working**:
   - Now that you have a local copy of the repository, you can start making changes. Use git add, git commit, and git push to manage your changes. If you don't have write access, you can push to your own fork or branch.
6. **Syncing Your Local Repository**:
   - To stay up to date with changes from the remote repository, you can run:

```css
git pull origin main
```

Real-World Example: Contributing to an Open-Source Project by Forking

Forking is particularly useful when you want to contribute to an open-source project. The typical workflow for contributing to open-source repositories is to **fork** the repository, make your changes in your own copy, and then submit those changes to the original repository using a **pull request**.

Scenario: Contributing to an Open-Source Project

Let's say you want to contribute to a popular open-source project called OpenWeatherApp. The project is hosted on GitHub, and you want to add a new feature, such as a dark mode toggle.

Step 1: Fork the Repository

1. **Go to the GitHub Repository**: Visit the OpenWeatherApp repository on GitHub.
2. **Fork the Repository**:
   - In the upper-right corner of the repository page, click on the **Fork** button. This creates a copy of the repository under your own GitHub account.
3. **Clone Your Fork Locally**:
   - Now that you have a fork, you need to clone it to your local machine to start working. Copy the URL of your fork (e.g., https://github.com/yourusername/OpenWeatherApp.git).
   - Run the following command in your terminal to clone your fork:

```bash
git clone https://github.com/yourusername/OpenWeatherApp.git
```

4. **Navigate into the Cloned Repository**:
   - Change to the directory of your cloned fork:

```bash
cd OpenWeatherApp
```

Step 2: Create a New Branch

Before making changes, it's a good practice to create a new branch for your feature or fix. This helps keep your changes isolated and easy to manage.

1. **Create a Feature Branch**:
   - Create a new branch called dark-mode:

```css
git checkout -b dark-mode
```

2. **Make Your Changes**:
   - Implement the dark mode feature in your local project. You might modify CSS, add JavaScript, or make other changes.
3. **Stage and Commit the Changes**:

- After making the changes, stage them:

  ```csharp
  git add .
  ```

- Then commit the changes:

  ```sql
  git commit -m "Add dark mode toggle feature"
  ```

Step 3: Push Changes to Your Fork

Once the feature is complete and committed, you need to push your changes to your forked repository on GitHub.

1. **Push Your Branch**:
   - Push the changes to your forked repository:

     ```perl
     git push origin dark-mode
     ```

2. **Create a Pull Request**:
   - After pushing the changes, go to your GitHub fork. You will see a prompt to create a pull request (PR) from your dark-mode branch to the original main branch of the OpenWeatherApp repository.

   - Click **New Pull Request** and follow the instructions to create a pull request.
3. **Review and Discuss**:
   - The project maintainers will review your pull request. They may request changes, ask questions, or merge your changes directly. If changes are requested, make them, commit the updates, and push them to your branch.
4. **Merge the Pull Request**:
   - Once the pull request is reviewed and approved, it will be merged into the original repository.

Step 4: Sync Your Fork with the Original Repository

As the original repository evolves, you may want to keep your fork up to date with the latest changes. Here's how to do that:

1. **Add the Original Repository as a Remote**:
   - Add the original repository (upstream) as a remote:

     csharp

     ```
     git remote add upstream https://github.com/original-owner/OpenWeatherApp.git
     ```

2. **Fetch the Latest Changes from the Original Repository**:
   - Fetch the changes from the original repository:

     sql

```
git fetch upstream
```

3. **Merge the Changes**:
   - Merge the changes into your local repository:

```css
git checkout main
git merge upstream/main
```

4. **Push Changes to Your Fork**:
   - Push the updated main branch to your fork:

```css
git push origin main
```

In this chapter, we learned about the difference between **cloning** and **forking** repositories:

- **Cloning** creates a local copy of a remote repository, typically used when you want to start working on a project directly.
- **Forking** creates a copy of a repository under your own GitHub account, which is used for contributing to open-

source projects without directly modifying the original codebase.

We also covered:

- How to **clone a repository** and start working with it locally.
- A **real-world example** of contributing to an open-source project by forking it, making changes, and submitting a pull request.

Now that you understand how to clone and fork repositories, you are ready to collaborate on open-source projects and manage your code effectively. In the next chapter, we will explore **advanced Git workflows**, such as using **rebase** and **cherry-pick** for more complex version control tasks.

Chapter 10: GitHub Basics

In this chapter, we will introduce **GitHub**, one of the most popular platforms for hosting Git repositories. We will walk you through the process of **creating your GitHub account**, setting up your GitHub profile, and highlight some of the platform's essential features that are commonly used by developers. We'll also dive into a real-world example to help you get started with your GitHub profile.

Introduction to GitHub as a Platform

GitHub is a web-based platform built around **Git**, a distributed version control system. It provides tools to help developers store, manage, and collaborate on code. GitHub adds a layer of collaboration to Git by offering a user-friendly interface that makes it easier to interact with Git repositories. It is used by millions of developers and is especially popular in the open-source community.

Key Features of GitHub:

1. **Repositories**:
   - GitHub allows you to host Git repositories, which are collections of your code, configuration files, and commit history. These repositories can be public (open-source) or private (restricted to specific collaborators).

2. **Version Control**:
   - GitHub is built on top of Git, meaning it supports all the version control features Git provides. This includes branching, merging, pull requests, and the ability to track and revert changes.
3. **Collaboration**:
   - GitHub makes it easy for multiple developers to collaborate on the same project. You can create **pull requests**, which allow others to review your code and suggest changes before merging it into the main project.
4. **Issues and Project Management**:
   - GitHub provides built-in tools for tracking bugs and managing tasks using **issues**. You can create, label, and assign issues, as well as associate them with commits or pull requests.
   - GitHub also offers **projects** (Kanban-style boards) for tracking the progress of tasks.
5. **GitHub Actions**:
   - GitHub offers **GitHub Actions**, a feature that allows you to automate your development workflows, such as running tests, building, and deploying code every time you push changes to your repository.
6. **Social and Community Features**:

   - GitHub enables social interaction among developers. You can **follow** other developers, **star** repositories, and **fork** projects to contribute to the open-source community.

7. **GitHub Pages**:
   - GitHub Pages is a feature that allows you to host static websites directly from a repository, making it easy to share your personal projects, documentation, or blogs.

Creating Your GitHub Account

To start using GitHub, the first step is to create an account. Here's how to do that:

Step 1: Go to GitHub's Sign-Up Page

- Navigate to https://github.com/join to create your GitHub account.

Step 2: Enter Your Information

- **Username**: Choose a unique username. This will be how others identify you on GitHub, and it's part of your profile URL (e.g., https://github.com/yourusername).
- **Email Address**: Enter your email address. This will be used for notifications and for logging into your account.

- **Password**: Choose a secure password to protect your account.
- **Verify Your Account**: GitHub will ask you to complete a CAPTCHA to verify you're not a bot.

Step 3: Choose Your Plan

- GitHub offers both free and paid plans. The free plan provides unlimited public repositories and limited private repositories. If you want to work with private repositories or use advanced features, you can opt for a paid plan.

Step 4: Customize Your Experience

- GitHub will ask you to choose a few preferences about how you plan to use the platform. You can skip this step if you wish.

Step 5: Verify Your Email

- Once your account is created, GitHub will send a verification email to the address you provided. Open your email inbox, click the verification link, and you'll be ready to start using GitHub!

Real-World Example: Setting Up Your GitHub Profile

After creating your GitHub account, the next step is to set up your profile. Your GitHub profile is where others can see your repositories, contributions, and activity. It's important to make your profile professional and informative, especially if you're looking to collaborate with others or showcase your work.

Step 1: Add a Profile Picture

- A profile picture helps personalize your GitHub account. Click on your profile picture in the top-right corner of GitHub, then select **Settings**. In the settings menu, you can upload a photo or avatar of yourself. This is optional but adds a personal touch.

Step 2: Edit Your Bio

- In your profile, you can edit your **bio** to give a brief introduction about yourself. You can include your skills, interests, and what you're working on. This is a great opportunity to provide a professional description that can make it easier for others to learn more about you.

Step 3: Add a Personal Website or Portfolio

- If you have a personal website, blog, or portfolio, add the URL to your profile. This is a great way to link to additional work or documentation. You can edit this in the **Profile** settings under **Website**.

Step 4: Customize Your Profile README

- GitHub allows you to add a **README** to your profile, which can be a more detailed introduction about yourself. To create this:
    - Create a new repository with the same name as your GitHub username (e.g., yourusername/yourusername).
    - Add a README.md file to this repository. This will display as the main content of your GitHub profile page.
    - You can include details like your projects, skills, and what you're working on. Use Markdown to format the text and add images, links, etc.

Step 5: Add Social Links

- GitHub allows you to link to your other social media profiles. Under the **Profile** settings, you can link to platforms like **Twitter**, **LinkedIn**, or **StackOverflow**, so people can easily connect with you across different platforms.

Step 6: Make Your Repositories Public or Private

- In your GitHub settings, you can choose the visibility of your repositories. By default, repositories are public, meaning anyone can view them. You can make a repository **private** if you want to restrict access to specific collaborators.

Step 7: Create Your First Repository

1. Go to the **Repositories** tab of your GitHub profile and click the **New** button to create your first repository.
2. Give it a name (e.g., my-first-repo), add a description, and choose whether to make it public or private.
3. Once created, you can follow the instructions to clone the repository, add files, and start working on it.

Additional Features of GitHub to Explore

1. **GitHub Gists**: Gists allow you to share code snippets, notes, or any other small text-based content with the public. They can be useful for sharing individual files or quick examples.
2. **GitHub Discussions**: Some repositories use **Discussions** for team communication or to answer questions. It's similar to a forum where community members can ask and answer questions, share ideas, or discuss topics related to a project.
3. **Contributing to Open-Source**: Once your profile is set up, you can start contributing to open-source projects. Look for

repositories that welcome contributions, check for the **Contributing.md** guidelines, and start by fixing issues or adding features.

In this chapter, we introduced **GitHub** as a powerful platform for hosting and collaborating on Git repositories. We covered:

- **Creating a GitHub account** and the steps to get started.
- **Setting up your GitHub profile**, including adding a profile picture, bio, website, and social links.
- A **real-world example** of setting up your GitHub profile, adding a README, and creating your first repository.

Now that your GitHub profile is set up, you're ready to begin hosting your projects, collaborating with others, and contributing to open-source. In the next chapter, we will explore **collaboration features** on GitHub, such as creating and managing pull requests, reviewing code, and working with teams.

Chapter 11: Collaborating with GitHub

In this chapter, we will explore how to collaborate using **GitHub**. Collaboration is one of GitHub's core strengths, and it offers several tools to make working with others easier and more organized. We'll cover key features like **issues**, **pull requests**, and **discussions**, and how you can use them to collaborate on projects effectively. We'll also provide a real-world example of reviewing and merging pull requests to demonstrate how collaboration flows in practice.

How to Collaborate Using GitHub

GitHub provides a variety of features that facilitate collaboration among developers, whether you're working on a small team or contributing to a large open-source project. Here are some key features of GitHub that make collaboration smooth and efficient:

1. Repositories and Branches for Teamwork

- GitHub repositories allow multiple developers to contribute to the same project by cloning the repository, creating feature branches, and then merging their changes back into the main project. Each team member works in isolation on their own branch, which prevents conflicts with others' work.

2. Forking and Pull Requests

- **Forking** a repository allows you to make a copy of another user's project, which you can modify independently. Once you've made changes, you can create a **pull request (PR)** to propose your changes to the original repository. This process is commonly used in open-source development, where contributors don't have write access to the original project.

3. Pull Requests and Code Review

- Pull requests are the backbone of collaboration on GitHub. They allow developers to submit their changes to be reviewed before they are merged into the main codebase. Reviewers can comment on the code, suggest changes, or approve the changes for merging.
- GitHub's **code review** feature allows developers to discuss specific lines of code, making collaboration more transparent and ensuring the quality of contributions.

4. Issues and Project Management

- **Issues** on GitHub are used to track tasks, bugs, enhancements, and discussions related to a project. Each issue can be assigned to a specific person, labeled (e.g., bug, enhancement, etc.), and commented on by other developers.
- Issues can also be linked to pull requests, making it easier to associate the changes with a specific task or bug.

5. GitHub Actions and CI/CD

- **GitHub Actions** allows you to automate workflows, including Continuous Integration (CI) and Continuous Deployment (CD). For example, you can set up actions to automatically run tests on your code whenever a pull request is submitted, ensuring that new changes do not break the project.

Issues, Pull Requests, and Discussions

1. Issues

GitHub issues are used for bug tracking, feature requests, and general project management. Issues provide a centralized location where you can discuss a problem or a feature before making changes to the code. Here's how issues are used:

- **Creating an Issue**: To create an issue, go to the **Issues** tab in a repository and click the **New Issue** button. You can provide a title, description, and label (e.g., bug, enhancement, question) to categorize the issue.
- **Assigning an Issue**: Issues can be assigned to one or more collaborators to indicate who is responsible for addressing them.

- **Commenting on Issues**: Team members can discuss the issue by commenting on it, suggesting solutions, or sharing their thoughts.

2. Pull Requests

Pull requests are the primary way to propose changes to a project. They allow you to submit code from your feature branch or fork to the main repository for review and eventual merging. Here's how pull requests work:

- **Creating a Pull Request**: To create a pull request, you first need to make changes in a branch and push those changes to the remote repository. Then, you can open a pull request (PR) from that branch to the main codebase (often the `main` or `master` branch).

  Once the PR is opened, you can add a title and description to explain the changes and link it to any related issues.

- **Reviewing a Pull Request**: Once a pull request is opened, collaborators can review the code changes. They can leave comments, ask questions, and request changes before the PR is merged.

  GitHub offers a feature to comment on specific lines of code in the pull request, making it easy to discuss individual changes.

- **Merging a Pull Request**: When the pull request is approved, the reviewer can merge the changes into the main codebase. Merging can be done with or without a fast-forward merge, depending on the repository settings.
- **Pull Request Workflow**: If changes are requested in the PR, the contributor can make additional commits to address the feedback. The PR will automatically update with the new changes.

3. Discussions

GitHub Discussions is a feature for long-term conversations within the project. It is useful for brainstorming ideas, asking questions, and sharing knowledge about the project. It differs from issues because it's intended for broader conversations, whereas issues are more focused on specific tasks or bugs.

Discussions can be organized by categories like:

- **General Discussion**: Open-ended conversations about the project.
- **Ideas and Proposals**: Discuss potential new features or changes to the project.
- **Q&A**: A place to ask and answer questions related to the project.

Real-World Example: Reviewing and Merging Pull Requests

Let's walk through an example where a developer submits a pull request, and another developer reviews and merges it.

Scenario: Alice Working on a New Feature

1. **Alice Forks and Clones the Repository**:
   - Alice wants to contribute to an open-source project called AwesomeApp. She forks the repository to her GitHub account and clones it to her local machine:

     bash

     ```
     git clone https://github.com/alice/awesomeapp.git
     ```

2. **Alice Creates a New Branch and Makes Changes**:
   - Alice creates a new feature branch called feature-login:

     css

     ```
     git checkout -b feature-login
     ```

   - She makes the necessary changes for the new login feature and commits them:

     sql

     ```
     git add .
     git commit -m "Implement login feature"
     ```

3. **Alice Pushes Her Changes to GitHub**:
   - Alice pushes the changes to her remote fork:

     ```perl
     git push origin feature-login
     ```

4. **Alice Opens a Pull Request**:
   - On GitHub, Alice opens a pull request from her `feature-login` branch to the `main` branch of the original repository.
   - She provides a detailed description of the changes she made and references the related issue in the project's repository.
5. **Bob Reviews the Pull Request**:
   - Bob is a maintainer of the `AwesomeApp` repository. He receives a notification about Alice's pull request.
   - Bob reviews the code changes by checking the **Files Changed** tab in the pull request. He notices that the login feature implementation is good but asks Alice to improve the error handling in case of invalid login attempts.
6. **Alice Updates the Pull Request**:
   - Alice reads Bob's feedback and improves the error handling by adding proper messages for invalid credentials.

  - She commits the changes and pushes them to the same branch:

    ```sql
    git add login.js
    git commit -m "Improve error handling for login"
    git push origin feature-login
    ```

7. **Bob Approves and Merges the Pull Request**:
   - Once Bob sees that the issue is fixed, he approves the pull request.
   - Bob merges the pull request into the `main` branch using GitHub's **Merge** button. This combines Alice's changes with the main project code.
8. **Closing the Pull Request**:
   - After merging, Bob closes the pull request. The feature is now part of the main codebase, and Alice's contribution is officially included in the project.

In this chapter, we explored how to **collaborate on GitHub** using key features like issues, pull requests, and discussions. We covered:

- **How to use GitHub issues** to track tasks and bugs, and how to organize project work.

- **Creating and reviewing pull requests**, including the process of submitting changes, reviewing code, and merging contributions.
- **Using GitHub Discussions** to foster open conversations around your project.

We also walked through a **real-world example** of reviewing and merging pull requests, which is a typical workflow when collaborating on open-source or team projects.

With these tools, you can collaborate efficiently with others, contribute to open-source projects, and keep your codebase clean and organized. In the next chapter, we will look at **advanced Git workflows** like rebasing and cherry-picking to handle more complex version control scenarios.

Chapter 12: Managing Multiple Branches

In this chapter, we will explore how to effectively **manage multiple branches** in a Git project. Working with multiple branches is a common scenario in software development, especially when working on new features, bug fixes, or experiments in parallel. We'll discuss how to handle multiple branches in a project, how to keep branches in sync with the main branch, and provide a **real-world example** of managing feature branches in a web development team.

How to Handle Multiple Branches in a Project

Branches are essential for maintaining clean workflows in Git. Each branch serves a specific purpose, such as working on a new feature, fixing a bug, or trying out an experimental idea. Here's how to handle multiple branches efficiently:

1. Create Feature or Bugfix Branches

When working on a project with multiple team members, it's a best practice to create separate branches for each feature or bugfix. This allows developers to work on different tasks independently without interfering with each other's work.

- To create a new branch:

css

```
git checkout -b feature-branch
```

- To switch between branches:

```
git checkout feature-branch
```

2. Naming Conventions

Using a consistent naming convention for branches is important for organization and clarity. Common naming patterns include:

- feature/<feature-name>: Used for new features.
- bugfix/<bug-name>: Used for fixing bugs.
- hotfix/<critical-issue>: Used for urgent fixes.
- experiment/<experiment-name>: Used for trying out new ideas.

For example:

- feature/login-form
- bugfix/fix-header-alignment

3. Keep Branches Focused

Each branch should have a specific purpose and focus. For example, if you're working on a login feature, don't include unrelated changes in the same branch, such as styling fixes or other UI changes. Keep your branches small, concise, and focused on one task.

Keeping Your Branches in Sync

As your project progresses, the main branch (or master) may receive updates, such as bug fixes, new features, or other important changes. It's important to keep your feature branches up to date with the main branch to avoid conflicts and ensure that your changes don't conflict with others'.

Here's how to keep your branches in sync with the main branch:

1. Syncing with the Latest Changes from Main

Before you start working on your feature branch, or after pulling the latest updates from main, it's crucial to ensure that your feature branch is up to date with any changes in main.

1. **Switch to the main branch**:

   css

   ```
   git checkout main
   ```

2. **Fetch the latest changes from the remote repository**:

   sql

   ```
   git fetch origin
   ```

3. **Merge changes into main**:

   bash

```
git merge origin/main
```

4. **Switch back to your feature branch**:

```
git checkout feature-login
```

5. **Merge main into your feature branch**:

```css
git merge main
```

This ensures that your feature branch contains the latest changes from the main branch, reducing the risk of merge conflicts when it's time to merge your changes back into main.

2. Rebase for a Cleaner History

Instead of merging main into your feature branch, some teams prefer to use **rebasing** to keep the project history cleaner and more linear.

1. **Switch to your feature branch**:

```
git checkout feature-login
```

2. **Rebase your branch on top of the latest main branch**:

css

```
git rebase main
```

3. If conflicts arise during the rebase, resolve them and continue the rebase:

```kotlin
git rebase --continue
```

Rebasing rewrites the history of your feature branch by placing your commits on top of the latest main branch. This creates a cleaner, linear commit history.

3. Deleting a Branch After Use

Once a branch is merged into the main branch and its work is complete, it's a good practice to delete the branch to keep the repository clean and organized.

- To delete a local branch:

```
git branch -d feature-login
```

- To delete a remote branch:

```perl
git push origin --delete feature-login
```

Deleting branches once they're no longer needed ensures that you don't have too many obsolete branches in the repository.

Real-World Example: Managing Feature Branches in a Web Development Team

Let's consider a real-world example where a **web development team** is working on a web app, and several developers are working on different features at the same time. In this scenario, each developer works on their own feature branch, and the team needs to keep the branches in sync with the main project.

Step 1: Setting Up the Project

1. The project is initialized with the main branch, which contains the base version of the website.
2. The team creates several feature branches:
    - feature/login-form
    - feature/navbar-improvements
    - feature/contact-page

Step 2: Developer A Works on the Login Form

1. **Developer A** starts by creating the feature/login-form branch and works on building the login page.

```css
git checkout -b feature/login-form
```

2. Developer A commits the changes and pushes the branch to the remote repository:

```
bash

git push origin feature/login-form
```

Step 3: Developer B Works on the Navbar Improvements

1. **Developer B** starts working on the feature/navbar-improvements branch.

```
bash

git checkout -b feature/navbar-improvements
```

2. Developer B makes UI changes to the navbar and commits the changes:

```
sql

git commit -m "Improve navbar layout and add dropdown"
```

3. Before pushing the changes, Developer B wants to ensure that their branch is in sync with the latest changes in main.
4. Developer B fetches and merges the latest changes from main:

```
css

git checkout main
```

```
git fetch origin
git merge origin/main
git checkout feature/navbar-improvements
git merge main
```

Step 4: Merging Feature Branches into Main

Once both feature branches are complete, **Developer A** and **Developer B** want to merge their work back into the main branch.

1. Developer A first ensures their feature/login-form branch is up to date with the latest changes from main:

   bash

   ```
   git checkout feature/login-form
   git fetch origin
   git merge origin/main
   ```

2. After resolving any conflicts, Developer A merges the feature branch into main:

   css

   ```
   git checkout main
   git merge feature/login-form
   git push origin main
   ```

3. Developer B does the same for their branch:

   bash

```
git checkout feature/navbar-improvements
git fetch origin
git merge origin/main
git checkout main
git merge feature/navbar-improvements
git push origin main
```

Step 5: Deleting the Feature Branches

Once the features are merged into main, the team deletes the feature branches to keep the repository organized:

- Developer A deletes the feature/login-form branch:

css

```
git branch -d feature/login-form
git push origin --delete feature/login-form
```

- Developer B deletes the feature/navbar-improvements branch:

bash

```
git branch -d feature/navbar-improvements
git push origin --delete feature/navbar-improvements
```

In this chapter, we explored how to **manage multiple branches** in Git, including:

- How to create feature branches and keep them isolated for different tasks.
- How to **keep branches in sync** with the main branch by using merge or rebase strategies.
- **Deleting branches** after they have been merged to keep your repository clean.

We also discussed a **real-world example** of a web development team managing feature branches, merging them into main, and keeping the branches synchronized to avoid conflicts.

Managing multiple branches is an essential skill for any developer working in a team, and mastering this process ensures efficient collaboration and a clean codebase. In the next chapter, we will explore **advanced Git workflows**, such as rebasing, cherry-picking, and handling complex merge conflicts.

Chapter 13: Best Practices for Commit Messages

In this chapter, we will discuss the importance of writing **clear, concise, and informative commit messages**. We'll explore **conventional commit standards**, which provide a structured way of writing commit messages to make version history more readable and understandable. We'll also review a **real-world example** of a project with a consistent and well-maintained commit history, which illustrates the power of well-written commit messages.

Writing Clear, Concise, and Informative Commit Messages

Commit messages are crucial for maintaining a clean and understandable history of your project. A well-written commit message helps other developers (and your future self) understand the reasoning behind changes without needing to dive into the code itself. Here's how you can write effective commit messages:

1. The Structure of a Good Commit Message

A good commit message should be structured, clear, and easy to understand. The typical structure includes the following components:

- **Title ()**: The first line of the commit message should be a brief of the changes, ideally 50-72 characters in length. It should describe **what** has been changed, and if possible, **why** the change was made.

- **Body (Optional, but Useful)**: After the title, leave a blank line and then provide a detailed explanation of the changes, especially if they are complex. The body can describe **why** the change was necessary, the problem it solves, or the broader context. The body should be wrapped at 72 characters for readability.

2. Best Practices for Writing Commit Messages

- **Use the imperative mood**: The commit message should be written as a command, like you're telling the system what to do. For example:
  - **Good**: "Fix bug in login form validation"
  - **Bad**: "Fixed bug in login form validation"

  The imperative mood matches the structure of Git commands like `git merge` or `git revert`, and it makes the history more consistent.

- **Keep it concise, but informative**: The title should summarize the changes, while the body (if included) should explain why the change was made. Avoid long, irrelevant descriptions.
- **Use the body for context**: If the commit involves complex or non-obvious changes, the body is a great place to explain

why certain decisions were made or how the change fits into the broader scope of the project. However, if the change is small and self-explanatory, a body might not be necessary.

- **Use issue references**: If the commit fixes an issue, include a reference to the issue number. This can help maintain context for the change. For example:

```sql
git commit -m "Fix crash on login page (fixes #42)"
```

3. Examples of Good Commit Messages

Here are a few examples of well-written commit messages:

- **Fixing bugs**: "Fix bug where user login fails on incorrect password"
- **Adding features**: "Add 'forgot password' functionality to login page"
- **Refactoring code**: "Refactor login form validation for readability"
- **Updating documentation**: "Update README with instructions for local setup"
- **Deleting code**: "Remove deprecated login method from auth module"

Understanding Conventional Commit Standards

To further standardize commit messages, many teams adopt **Conventional Commits**—a convention that prescribes a consistent format for commit messages. This helps create an easily understandable and navigable commit history.

Conventional Commit Format

The standard format for a conventional commit message is:

```php
<type>(<scope>): <message>
```

- **type**: A short descriptor of the type of change (e.g., feat, fix, chore).
- **scope** (optional): A brief description of the area of the codebase the change pertains to (e.g., auth, ui, api).
- **message**: A concise description of the change.

Types of Commits

Some commonly used types in conventional commits include:

- **feat**: A new feature or enhancement.
- **fix**: A bug fix.
- **docs**: Documentation changes.
- **style**: Code formatting, such as fixing indentation or adding new lines (without changing the actual logic).
- **refactor**: Code changes that neither fix a bug nor add a feature, but make the code cleaner or more maintainable.

- **test**: Adding or updating tests.
- **chore**: Changes to the build process or auxiliary tools (e.g., dependency updates, formatting changes).

Examples of Conventional Commit Messages

- feat(auth): add login form validation
- fix(ui): resolve navbar overlapping on mobile
- docs(readme): update API usage examples
- chore(deps): update dependencies to latest versions

Benefits of Conventional Commits

1. **Consistency**: Having a consistent format makes it easier to understand the history of a project. When every commit follows the same structure, it becomes much easier to skim through the log and see what changes have been made.
2. **Automated Changelog Generation**: Tools like **semantic-release** can automatically generate changelogs based on commit messages. By following the Conventional Commit format, your team can automate the process of tracking what features or fixes have been added in each release.
3. **Easier Collaboration**: With standardized commit messages, all team members (and contributors) know how to write commits and understand the meaning of different types of changes.

Real-World Example: A Project with a Consistent Commit History

Let's consider a **real-world example** of a project with a consistent commit history. Imagine a team of developers working on a **web application** called "TaskMaster," a task management app. They follow a well-defined commit message convention.

Example 1: Adding a New Feature

Developer Alice adds a new feature to allow users to create tasks with deadlines. She creates a feature branch called feature/task-deadline and commits her work.

Commit message:

```scss
feat(task): add deadline functionality for tasks
```

This commit clearly indicates that a new feature was added (a deadline functionality for tasks), and the scope (task) specifies which part of the application the feature is related to.

Example 2: Fixing a Bug

Developer Bob works on fixing a bug where the app crashes when a user tries to delete a task. He creates a branch called bugfix/task-delete-crash and commits the fix.

Commit message:

```scss
fix(task): resolve crash when deleting tasks
```

This message indicates that a bug was fixed, and the scope clearly mentions that it's related to the task feature.

Example 3: Updating Documentation

Developer Charlie updates the README to explain how to set up the application locally. He commits his changes.

Commit message:

```scss
docs(readme): update setup instructions for local dev
```

This commit message indicates that the change is documentation-related, and the scope (readme) specifies which part of the documentation was updated.

Example 4: Refactoring Code

Developer Dave refactors the authentication module to make it more efficient. He commits the changes.

Commit message:

```scss
refactor(auth): improve login flow for better user experience
```

This commit message specifies that the change is a **refactor** (not adding a feature or fixing a bug), and the scope is auth, indicating that the authentication system was the focus.

In this chapter, we learned the importance of writing **clear, concise, and informative commit messages**. We discussed:

- **Best practices** for commit messages, including using the imperative mood, being concise, and providing context in the body.
- **Conventional Commit standards**, which provide a consistent format for commit messages, helping teams maintain a clean and understandable commit history.
- A **real-world example** of a project with a consistent commit history, showing how teams use meaningful commit messages to make their codebase more manageable and easier to navigate.

By following these best practices, you can ensure that your project's commit history is clear, professional, and easy to follow, which is especially important when working on large teams or contributing to open-source projects. In the next chapter, we will explore **advanced Git techniques** for managing complex project workflows and solving issues that may arise during development.

Chapter 14: Advanced Git Commands

In this chapter, we will explore some **advanced Git commands** that can help you manage your repository more effectively. These commands—**git reset**, **git rebase**, and **git cherry-pick**—are useful in various situations where you need to undo changes, rewrite history, or apply changes from one branch to another. Understanding when and how to use these commands is essential for maintaining a clean Git history and handling complex scenarios.

Exploring git reset, git rebase, and git cherry-pick

1. git reset

The git reset command is one of the most powerful and potentially dangerous commands in Git. It is used to **undo changes** in your repository, and it can modify the commit history in several ways. There are three primary types of reset:

- **Soft Reset**: This moves the HEAD pointer to a previous commit but leaves your working directory and staging area unchanged.

  css

  ```
  git reset --soft <commit>
  ```

This is useful when you want to **undo a commit** but keep the changes in your staging area, so you can recommit them.

- **Mixed Reset (default)**: This resets the HEAD pointer and the staging area to a previous commit but leaves your working directory unchanged. This is the default behavior when you use git reset without any flags.

  perl

  ```
  git reset <commit>
  ```

  This is useful when you want to **unstage files** that were added previously but keep the changes in your working directory.

- **Hard Reset**: This completely resets your repository, including the working directory and the staging area, to a specific commit. Any changes since that commit will be **lost**.

  css

  ```
  git reset --hard <commit>
  ```

  This is useful when you want to **discard all changes** and revert to a clean state at a specific commit.

2. git rebase

The git rebase command is used to **reapply commits** from one branch onto another. It allows you to **rewrite commit history** by changing the base of your branch, creating a cleaner and more linear history. It is commonly used to integrate the latest changes from the main branch into your feature branch or to squash multiple commits into a single commit.

- **Interactive Rebase**: You can use git rebase -i (interactive rebase) to perform more complex history rewrites, such as squashing commits, reordering commits, or editing commit messages.

  css

  ```
  git rebase -i <commit>
  ```

  This opens an interactive editor where you can specify how to manipulate the commits in your history. For example, you can **squash** commits (combine them into one), **edit** commit messages, or even **drop** commits entirely.

- **Rebase vs. Merge**: While merging creates a merge commit, git rebase moves the base of the branch and applies the commits from the feature branch one by one on top of the target branch (usually main). This results in a linear commit history, without merge commits.

  css

  ```
  git rebase main
  ```

This will rebase your current branch on top of the main branch.

3. git cherry-pick

The git cherry-pick command is used to **apply changes from a specific commit** onto your current branch. It allows you to selectively apply commits from other branches or even from the same branch. This is useful when you want to apply a fix from one branch without merging all changes from that branch.

- **Basic Usage**:

  php

  ```
  git cherry-pick <commit-hash>
  ```

  This will apply the changes from the specified commit to your current branch, creating a new commit.

- **Handling Conflicts**: Like with merging, if there are conflicts during a cherry-pick operation, you will need to resolve them before finalizing the cherry-pick.

When to Use These Advanced Commands

Each of these commands is suited to different scenarios in your workflow. Here's when you might use each of them:

1. git reset

- **Undoing a Commit (Soft Reset)**: If you commit something by mistake or realize that you need to make changes before committing, use git reset --soft to uncommit the changes but keep them staged.
- **Unstaging Files (Mixed Reset)**: If you accidentally staged files with git add but haven't committed yet, use git reset to unstage the files without affecting your working directory.
- **Completely Discarding Changes (Hard Reset)**: If you want to completely discard any local changes and reset your project to a clean state, use git reset --hard. Be careful, as this will erase any uncommitted changes in your working directory.

2. git rebase

- **Keeping Your Branch Up to Date**: If you are working on a feature branch and want to integrate the latest changes from the main branch into your branch, use git rebase main to rebase your changes on top of the updated main branch. This keeps the history clean and linear.
- **Squashing Commits**: If your feature branch has multiple commits that can be combined into one, use git rebase -i to squash them. This reduces clutter in the commit history.
- **Rewriting History**: If you need to rewrite commit history, such as modifying commit messages, changing commit order, or dropping commits, use git rebase -i.

3. git cherry-pick

- **Applying Specific Changes**: If you need to apply a specific fix or feature from one branch to another without merging the entire branch, use git cherry-pick. For example, if a bug was fixed in a feature branch and you want that fix in the main branch, you can cherry-pick that commit.
- **Isolating Commits**: Use git cherry-pick to apply changes to multiple branches or to selectively introduce changes to a branch.

Real-World Example: Fixing a Commit History with git rebase

Let's consider a real-world example of using git rebase to fix a messy commit history. Imagine you're working on a project with a few collaborators. You've been working on a feature branch and have made several small commits, but the commit history looks messy and disorganized. Some commits are too granular, while others could be combined.

Step 1: Inspect the Commit History

You run the following command to view the commit history on your feature branch:

```lua
git log --oneline
```

You see a history like this:

```sql
abc1234 Add validation to user input
def5678 Fix typo in validation message
ghi7890 Refactor input validation function
jkl0123 Add user input tests
```

While the changes are good, the commit history is not ideal. The first two commits are related to the same feature, and the commit messages could be improved.

Step 2: Interactive Rebase

To clean up the history, you start an interactive rebase:

```css
git rebase -i HEAD~4
```

This command tells Git to rebase the last four commits. The interactive editor opens, showing a list of commits:

```sql
pick abc1234 Add validation to user input
pick def5678 Fix typo in validation message
pick ghi7890 Refactor input validation function
pick jkl0123 Add user input tests
```

Step 3: Squash and Edit Commits

You decide to squash the first two commits (because they are related to the same feature) and modify the commit message for the squashed commit.

Change the rebase instructions to:

```sql
pick abc1234 Add validation to user input
squash def5678 Fix typo in validation message
pick ghi7890 Refactor input validation function
pick jkl0123 Add user input tests
```

After saving and closing the editor, Git will combine the two commits and ask you to edit the commit message. You modify it to:

```css
Add validation to user input and fix typo in validation message
```

Step 4: Complete the Rebase

After you've edited the commit message, Git will continue the rebase. If there are any conflicts (e.g., if the changes affect the same lines of code), you'll need to resolve them manually.

Once the rebase is complete, you'll have a cleaner commit history:

```sql
abc1234 Add validation to user input and fix typo in validation message
ghi7890 Refactor input validation function
jkl0123 Add user input tests
```

Step 5: Push the Changes

If the feature branch has already been pushed to the remote repository, you will need to force-push the changes after the rebase, since the history has been rewritten:

```css
git push origin feature-branch --force
```

This will update the remote repository with the new, cleaner commit history.

In this chapter, we explored three powerful Git commands: **git reset**, **git rebase**, and **git cherry-pick**. These commands help you manage and manipulate your Git history more effectively:

- **git reset** is used to undo changes and reset the repository to a previous state.
- **git rebase** is used to apply changes from one branch onto another, rewrite commit history, and keep a clean and linear history.
- **git cherry-pick** is used to apply individual commits from one branch to another.

We also looked at a **real-world example** of using `git rebase` to clean up a commit history, making it easier to navigate and understand.

By mastering these advanced Git commands, you can handle more complex workflows and ensure your Git history remains clean and manageable, which is especially important when working with teams or contributing to open-source projects. In the next chapter, we will explore how to manage **conflict resolution** and ensure smooth merging when collaborating with others.

Chapter 15: Understanding and Using Git Tags

In this chapter, we will explore **Git tags**, which are a powerful feature in Git for marking specific points in the commit history. Tags are commonly used to indicate releases, milestones, or other important events in a project's lifecycle. We'll discuss **what tags are, why they are important**, and how to **create and manage tags** in Git. We will also walk through a **real-world example** of tagging release versions in a project, which is a common use case for tags.

What Are Git Tags and Why Are They Important?

A **Git tag** is a reference to a specific commit in the Git history. Unlike branches, which are typically used for ongoing development, tags represent fixed points in the history, often used to mark **important events** such as:

- **Release versions** (e.g., v1.0, v2.0)
- **Milestones** in the project (e.g., beta releases)
- **Stable points** in the code (e.g., post-deployment)

Tags are useful for several reasons:

1. Marking Release Points

Tags are commonly used to mark **release versions** of a project. For example, when a software project reaches a stable version, you can tag that commit to easily refer back to it. This is particularly important in release management, where it's crucial to know the exact commit that corresponds to a specific version of the product.

2. Easier Navigation

Tags allow you to quickly navigate to important points in your project's history. If you want to check out the code at a specific release or milestone, you can simply check out the tag rather than searching through commit logs.

3. Versioning and Distribution

Tags are often used in conjunction with tools like **GitHub Releases**, where each tag represents a version that is associated with a downloadable release. Tags help in **version control**, making it clear which version of the software is being distributed.

4. Clarity for Collaboration

Tags provide clarity when working on collaborative projects. If your team is working on versioned software, tagging commits makes it clear which commits represent released versions, ensuring that everyone is on the same page.

Creating and Managing Tags

Git provides several commands for creating and managing tags. There are two main types of tags in Git:

1. Lightweight Tags

A lightweight tag is like a branch that doesn't change—it's simply a pointer to a specific commit. It's often used for personal use or quick references.

- **Creating a lightweight tag**:

```php
git tag <tag-name>
```

For example, to create a tag v1.0 for the current commit:

```
git tag v1.0
```

2. Annotated Tags

An annotated tag is a full Git object. It contains not only the commit hash but also the tagger's name, email, date, and a message. Annotated tags are the most common type of tag used to mark releases because they provide more information.

- **Creating an annotated tag**:

arduino

```
git tag -a <tag-name> -m "Tag message"
```

For example, to create an annotated tag v1.0 with a message:

```arduino
git tag -a v1.0 -m "First stable release"
```

3. Listing Tags

To list all the tags in a repository, use the git tag command:

```
git tag
```

This will display all the tags in your repository.

4. Viewing Tag Details

To view more information about a specific tag, such as the commit it points to, use the git show command:

```php
git show <tag-name>
```

For example:

```sql
git show v1.0
```

This will display information about the commit that the tag v1.0 points to, including the commit hash, author, date, and the tag message.

5. Pushing Tags to Remote

By default, tags are not automatically pushed to the remote repository when you push commits. To push tags to the remote repository, use the following command:

```perl
git push origin <tag-name>
```

For example:

```perl
git push origin v1.0
```

To push all tags to the remote repository:

```css
git push --tags
```

6. Deleting Tags

If you need to delete a tag, you can remove it locally and remotely.

- **Delete a tag locally**:

  ```php
  git tag -d <tag-name>
  ```

  For example:

  ```
  git tag -d v1.0
  ```

- **Delete a tag remotely**:

  perl

  ```
  git push --delete origin <tag-name>
  ```

  For example:

  perl

  ```
  git push --delete origin v1.0
  ```

Real-World Example: Tagging Release Versions in a Project

Let's walk through a **real-world example** of tagging release versions in a software project.

Step 1: Preparing for a Release

Imagine you're working on a web application project, and you're about to release version 1.0. All the development work has been completed, and the application is ready for release. Here's how you would tag the release version:

1. **Commit the final changes** for the release: Before tagging, make sure all the changes have been committed. For example:

   sql

   ```
   git add .
   ```

```
git commit -m "Prepare for version 1.0 release"
```

2. **Create an annotated tag for version 1.0**: Create a tag with a message indicating that this is the first stable release:

```arduino
git tag -a v1.0 -m "First stable release"
```

3. **Push the tag to the remote repository**: Push the tag to the remote repository so others can access it:

```perl
git push origin v1.0
```

Step 2: Working with Multiple Releases

As time progresses, the project will have multiple releases. Each new version can be tagged similarly. For example, when the application reaches version 1.1 with new features or bug fixes:

1. **Commit the changes for version 1.1**:

```sql
git add .
git commit -m "Add new features and bug fixes for version 1.1"
```

2. **Tag version 1.1**:

```arduino
git tag -a v1.1 -m "Version 1.1 with new features"
```

3. **Push the new tag to the remote repository**:

```perl
git push origin v1.1
```

Step 3: Viewing and Accessing Releases

Once the tags have been created, you can easily check out the code at any given release point. For example, if you want to check out version 1.0 of the project, you can do so using the tag:

```
git checkout v1.0
```

This will update your working directory to the state of the code at the time of the version 1.0 release.

Step 4: Tagging a Hotfix or Critical Release

If you need to create a hotfix (e.g., version 1.0.1) to address a critical bug in production, you can create a new tag on top of the latest stable version:

1. **Create a hotfix branch from the latest stable version**:

```css
git checkout -b hotfix-v1.0.1 v1.0
```

2. **Make the necessary fixes** for the hotfix and commit them:

```sql
git add .
git commit -m "Fix critical bug in user authentication"
```

3. **Tag the hotfix release**:

```arduino
git tag -a v1.0.1 -m "Hotfix for version 1.0"
```

4. **Push the hotfix tag to the remote repository**:

```perl
git push origin v1.0.1
```

Now, version 1.0.1 is tagged and available for anyone to reference, and the hotfix can be deployed to production.

In this chapter, we covered **Git tags**, including their types, uses, and commands for creating, managing, and deleting tags. Tags are important for marking specific points in your project's history, such as release versions or milestones. Here's what we learned:

- **Git tags** allow you to mark specific commits in your history with meaningful labels.
- **Annotated tags** are the most commonly used type, as they include additional metadata such as the author and message.
- **Managing tags** involves creating, viewing, pushing, and deleting tags to keep track of important milestones.
- A **real-world example** showed how to use tags for versioning and marking releases in a project.

Tags are a powerful tool for managing versions and releases in your project, making it easier to track changes, deploy software, and collaborate with others. In the next chapter, we will explore **Git workflows** and how to handle more complex project management tasks using Git.

Chapter 16: Git Stash and Temporary Changes

In this chapter, we will explore the powerful **git stash** command, which allows you to save and temporarily set aside your unfinished work. This can be incredibly helpful when you need to switch contexts or tasks without committing changes you're not ready to finalize. We'll cover when to use **git stash**, how to retrieve stashed changes, and provide a **real-world example** of using git stash when switching tasks in a development workflow.

Using git stash to Save Unfinished Work

In Git, when you're working on a feature or fix and you're interrupted (for example, you need to switch to another task), you may not be ready to commit your changes. In such cases, **git stash** comes in handy. It allows you to save your changes (both staged and unstaged) temporarily without committing them, so you can easily retrieve and continue working later.

How git stash Works

When you use git stash, Git saves your changes in a special stack and reverts the working directory to the state of the last commit. This allows you to switch to a different task without losing your progress.

You can retrieve your stashed changes later and continue working on them as if you never left.

Basic git stash Commands

1. **Stashing Changes**: To save your changes and revert your working directory to the last commit:

   ```
   git stash
   ```
   This saves both staged and unstaged changes.

2. **Stashing Only Unstaged Changes**: If you only want to stash changes that have not been staged (i.e., changes in the working directory), use:

   css

   ```
   git stash --keep-index
   ```
   This stashes only the changes that are not yet staged.

3. **Stashing Only Staged Changes**: To stash only the staged changes, you can use:

   css

   ```
   git stash --staged
   ```
   This stashes only the changes that have been added to the staging area.

4. **Saving a Stash with a Custom Message**: You can add a message to your stash to make it easier to remember later:

arduino

```
git stash save "message describing the work"
```

Listing Stashed Changes

To view a list of all stashed changes:

```
git stash list
```

This will show a list of stashes in your repository. Each stash is identified by a name like stash@{0}, stash@{1}, etc.

Applying Stashed Changes

When you're ready to retrieve your stashed changes and continue working on them, you can apply the stash:

1. **Applying the Most Recent Stash**:

   ```
   git stash apply
   ```

   This applies the most recent stash, but does not remove it from the stash list.

2. **Applying a Specific Stash**: If you have multiple stashes, you can specify which stash to apply by using its identifier (e.g., stash@{1}):

kotlin

git stash apply stash@{1}

Removing a Stash

Once you've applied a stash and no longer need it, you can remove it from the stash list:

1. **Removing the Most Recent Stash**:

   sql

   git stash drop

2. **Removing a Specific Stash**:

   kotlin

   git stash drop stash@{1}

3. **Clearing All Stashes**: To remove all stashed changes:

   arduino

   git stash clear

Pop a Stash

git stash pop applies the most recent stash and then removes it from the stash list:

perl

git stash pop

This command is equivalent to running git stash apply followed by git stash drop.

When to Stash and How to Retrieve Changes

When to Use git stash

git stash is useful in scenarios where you need to temporarily save your work without committing it. Some common situations include:

1. **Switching Tasks**: You are working on a feature but need to urgently fix a bug or work on something else. Instead of committing unfinished work, you can stash it and switch to the other task.
2. **Experimenting with Code**: When trying out experimental changes, you can stash your current work, make the experimental changes, and then either commit or discard them later without affecting your main work.
3. **Unfinished Work**: If you're in the middle of a task but need to quickly change branches, you can stash your current changes and apply them later once you're back to working on the original task.

How to Retrieve Stashed Changes

You can retrieve your stashed changes by using `git stash apply` or `git stash pop`. Use these commands when you're ready to continue working on the changes you saved earlier.

- **Apply a specific stash**:

  kotlin

  ```
  git stash apply stash@{0}
  ```

- **Pop the most recent stash**:

  perl

  ```
  git stash pop
  ```

- **Check the contents of a stash**: To see what's inside a stash before applying it:

  kotlin

  ```
  git stash show stash@{0}
  ```

You can also use the `-p` flag to display the diff of the changes:

css

```
git stash show -p stash@{0}
```

Real-World Example: Switching Tasks While Working on a Feature

Let's walk through a **real-world example** where a developer is working on a feature and needs to switch tasks temporarily.

Step 1: Working on the Feature

Imagine you're working on a feature that involves creating a new user registration form. You've made progress, but now you need to quickly fix a bug in the login feature. However, the user registration form is not ready for commit, and you don't want to commit half-finished work.

1. **You've made changes**, but you're not ready to commit them yet:
   - Added HTML for the form.
   - Modified some CSS.

Step 2: Stashing Your Changes

To temporarily save your work and switch tasks, you use git stash to save the current state:

```
git stash
```

This command saves both staged and unstaged changes and reverts your working directory back to the last commit, allowing you to work on something else.

Step 3: Switching to the Bug Fix Branch

Next, you switch to the bugfix/login-error branch to work on the bug:

```bash
git checkout bugfix/login-error
```

You can now fix the bug in the login feature, commit the changes, and push them to the remote repository.

Step 4: Returning to the Feature

After you've completed the bug fix and pushed the changes, you return to the feature branch to continue working on the user registration form.

1. **Switch back to the feature branch**:

   ```bash
   git checkout feature/user-registration
   ```

2. **Retrieve the stashed changes** using git stash pop:

   ```perl
   git stash pop
   ```

This command restores your changes and removes the stash, allowing you to continue working on the user registration form where you left off.

Step 5: Finalizing the Feature

Once you're done with the feature, you can commit the changes:

```sql
git add .
git commit -m "Add user registration form"
```

In this chapter, we learned about **git stash** and how it can be used to save unfinished work temporarily. We covered:

- **How to stash changes**, including using `git stash` for saving your work and `git stash apply` or `git stash pop` to retrieve it later.
- **When to use git stash**, such as when switching tasks or experimenting with code without committing unfinished changes.
- A **real-world example** of how to use `git stash` to temporarily save work, switch tasks, and then return to your original task.

`git stash` is a powerful tool that helps maintain your workflow without committing half-finished work. In the next chapter, we will dive into more advanced Git workflows and strategies for handling complex projects and collaborative development.

Chapter 17: Leveraging GitHub Actions for CI/CD

In this chapter, we will explore **GitHub Actions**, a feature of GitHub that allows you to automate workflows such as **Continuous Integration (CI)** and **Continuous Deployment (CD)**. We will walk through the process of setting up CI/CD pipelines, explain how workflows and actions work, and provide a **real-world example** of automating deployment using GitHub Actions.

Setting Up Continuous Integration and Deployment

Continuous Integration (CI) and **Continuous Deployment (CD)** are essential practices in modern software development. CI ensures that new code changes integrate smoothly with the existing codebase, and CD automates the deployment of that code to production environments.

GitHub Actions makes it easy to automate these processes by providing a way to define workflows directly in your repository. These workflows can be triggered by events such as **pushes**, **pull requests**, or on a scheduled basis.

1. Setting Up Continuous Integration with GitHub Actions

To set up CI, you'll define a **workflow** that runs your tests automatically whenever code is pushed to your repository. This ensures that new code changes don't break the application.

- **Step 1: Create a Workflow File** Workflows are defined in YAML files inside the .github/workflows/ directory in your repository. To set up CI, you'll need to create a new YAML file (e.g., ci.yml) inside the .github/workflows/ directory.

  Example: .github/workflows/ci.yml

  yaml

```
name: CI Workflow

on:
  push:
    branches:
      - main
  pull_request:
    branches:
      - main

jobs:
  build:
    runs-on: ubuntu-latest

    steps:
      - name: Checkout code
        uses: actions/checkout@v2
```

```
- name: Set up Node.js
  uses: actions/setup-node@v2
  with:
    node-version: '14'

- name: Install dependencies
  run: npm install

- name: Run tests
  run: npm test
```

- **Step 2: Define Workflow Triggers** The on field defines the events that will trigger the workflow. In the example above, the workflow is triggered by a push or a pull_request event to the main branch. You can customize this to fit your project's needs, such as running tests on feature branches or specific tags.
- **Step 3: Running Tests** The example workflow installs dependencies (npm install) and runs tests (npm test). You can adapt this for your project by using the appropriate commands to build and test your code.

2. Setting Up Continuous Deployment with GitHub Actions

Once your CI workflow is set up, you can extend it to **automate the deployment process** using GitHub Actions. This involves creating a deployment pipeline that deploys the application whenever a new release is tagged or a commit is pushed to a specific branch (e.g., main).

- **Step 1: Add Deployment Steps to Your Workflow** You can add deployment steps after the testing steps. For example, you can deploy your application to a cloud platform like **Heroku**, **AWS**, or **Azure**. The specific steps depend on the platform you're using.

  Example for deploying to **Heroku**:

  yaml

```yaml
name: Deploy to Heroku

on:
  push:
    branches:
      - main

jobs:
  deploy:
    runs-on: ubuntu-latest

    steps:
      - name: Checkout code
        uses: actions/checkout@v2

      - name: Set up Node.js
        uses: actions/setup-node@v2
```

```
    with:
      node-version: '14'

  - name: Install dependencies
    run: npm install

  - name: Run tests
    run: npm test

  - name: Deploy to Heroku
    uses: akshnz/heroku-deploy-action@v1.0
    with:
      heroku_api_key: ${{ secrets.HEROKU_API_KEY }}
      app_name: your-heroku-app-name
      branch: main
```

In this example, after the tests are successfully run, the code is deployed to **Heroku** using a specific action (akshnz/heroku-deploy-action). The Heroku API key is stored securely in GitHub's **Secrets** (to keep it private and secure).

- **Step 2: Use Secrets for Secure Information** You can store sensitive information like API keys, access tokens, or credentials in GitHub Secrets. This keeps your keys safe from being exposed in your workflow files.
  - Navigate to your repository settings, select **Secrets**, and add your sensitive information there (e.g., HEROKU_API_KEY).

Understanding Workflows and Actions

GitHub Actions are based on **workflows**, **jobs**, and **steps**. Let's break down how these components work:

1. Workflows

- A **workflow** is an automated process defined in a YAML file (like ci.yml or deploy.yml) that can be triggered by events like a push to a branch, a pull request, or even a manual trigger.
- Each workflow can contain multiple jobs.

2. Jobs

- A **job** is a collection of steps that run on the same runner. Each job is executed independently. Jobs can run in parallel, or you can set dependencies to ensure they run sequentially.
- For example, one job might be responsible for running tests, and another job might handle deployment.

3. Steps

- A **step** is an individual task in a job. Each step can run commands or use actions. Steps are executed sequentially within a job.
- You can use actions as steps to perform common tasks, such as checking out code or deploying to a platform.

4. Actions

- **Actions** are reusable units of work in GitHub Actions. These can be created by GitHub or the community and are shared via the GitHub marketplace. For example, actions can handle tasks like setting up Node.js, deploying to a cloud provider, or sending notifications.
- You can use actions in your workflows by specifying them in the `uses` field within a step.

Real-World Example: Automating Deployment Using GitHub Actions

Let's walk through a **real-world example** of setting up CI/CD for a web application project. In this example, we'll use **GitHub Actions** to automate testing and deployment to **Heroku**.

Step 1: Setup CI Workflow for Testing

1. Create a `.github/workflows/ci.yml` file in your repository:

```yaml
name: CI Workflow

on:
  push:
    branches:
```

```
      - main
  pull_request:
    branches:
      - main

jobs:
  build:
    runs-on: ubuntu-latest

    steps:
      - name: Checkout code
        uses: actions/checkout@v2

      - name: Set up Node.js
        uses: actions/setup-node@v2
        with:
          node-version: '14'

      - name: Install dependencies
        run: npm install

      - name: Run tests
        run: npm test
```

2. This workflow will run whenever there is a push or pull request to the `main` branch, automatically installing dependencies and running tests.

Step 2: Setup CD Workflow for Deployment

Once the tests are successful, you can add deployment to Heroku. Create a .github/workflows/deploy.yml file:

```yaml
name: Deploy to Heroku

on:
  push:
    branches:
      - main

jobs:
  deploy:
    runs-on: ubuntu-latest

    steps:
      - name: Checkout code
        uses: actions/checkout@v2

      - name: Set up Node.js
        uses: actions/setup-node@v2
        with:
          node-version: '14'

      - name: Install dependencies
        run: npm install

      - name: Run tests
        run: npm test
```

```
- name: Deploy to Heroku
  uses: akshnz/heroku-deploy-action@v1.0
  with:
    heroku_api_key: ${{ secrets.HEROKU_API_KEY }}
    app_name: your-heroku-app-name
    branch: main
```

1. After running tests, the workflow deploys your app to Heroku using a secure Heroku API key stored in GitHub Secrets (HEROKU_API_KEY).

Step 3: Secure Secrets for Deployment

1. Go to your GitHub repository settings.
2. In the **Secrets** section, add the HEROKU_API_KEY secret to securely store your Heroku API key.
3. With the secret stored, the deployment will be automatically handled each time there's a push to the main branch.

In this chapter, we covered **GitHub Actions** and how they can be used to automate **Continuous Integration (CI)** and **Continuous Deployment (CD)**. We explored:

- **How to set up workflows and actions** to automate tasks such as testing and deployment.

- **The structure of a workflow** in GitHub Actions, including jobs, steps, and actions.
- A **real-world example** of automating deployment to **Heroku** after running tests.

GitHub Actions simplifies the process of integrating and deploying your code, saving time and reducing the risk of errors. In the next chapter, we will dive deeper into more advanced GitHub Actions features, including caching dependencies and building custom actions.

Chapter 18: Security and Access Control on GitHub

In this chapter, we will discuss **security and access control** on GitHub, which are crucial for managing who can access your repositories and ensuring that your codebase remains secure. We'll cover topics such as **managing collaborators and teams, securing your repository with SSH keys**, and provide a **real-world example** of managing access to a private repository.

Managing Collaborators and Teams on GitHub

GitHub provides various tools to manage access to your repositories, particularly for collaborative projects. You can control who has access to your repositories by adding **collaborators** to individual repositories or by creating **teams** within an organization.

1. Managing Collaborators on a Repository

A **collaborator** is someone who has direct access to your repository, allowing them to read from and write to the repository. This is commonly used for personal projects or small teams.

- **Adding a Collaborator**:
  1. Go to your repository on GitHub.
  2. Click on the **Settings** tab.
  3. In the left sidebar, click **Collaborators & teams**.

4. Under the **Collaborators** section, enter the GitHub username of the person you want to add.
5. Click **Add collaborator** and send an invite. The user will receive an email and can accept the invite.

- **Removing a Collaborator**: To remove a collaborator, go to the same **Collaborators & teams** section in the repository settings, and you'll see a list of added collaborators. Click **Remove** next to the collaborator you want to remove.

2. Managing Teams on GitHub (for Organizations)

If you're working with an organization or a larger team, GitHub allows you to create **teams** to group members and manage access more effectively.

- **Creating a Team**:
  1. In your GitHub organization, go to **Settings**.
  2. Click on **Teams** in the left sidebar.
  3. Click **New team** and provide a name for the team (e.g., Dev Team, QA Team).
  4. Add members to the team by selecting their usernames.
  5. Set the team's permissions (e.g., **Read**, **Write**, or **Admin**) for the repositories they will access.
- **Assigning Team Access to Repositories**: You can assign a team access to one or more repositories in your organization.

Go to the **Repositories** section of the team settings and select which repositories the team should have access to.

3. Repository Permissions and Access Levels

For each collaborator or team, you can set specific repository access levels:

- **Read**: View and clone the repository.
- **Write**: Read, write, and push to the repository.
- **Admin**: Full control over the repository, including changing settings and managing collaborators.

By assigning the appropriate permissions, you can ensure that the right people have the right level of access.

Securing Your Repository with SSH Keys

When working with Git and GitHub, it's important to secure your access to the repositories, especially if you're pushing and pulling code regularly. **SSH keys** are a secure way to authenticate with GitHub, eliminating the need for entering your password each time you interact with a remote repository.

1. What Are SSH Keys?

SSH (Secure Shell) keys are a pair of cryptographic keys used to authenticate your identity when interacting with GitHub. The key pair consists of:

- A **private key**, which you keep on your local machine.
- A **public key**, which is uploaded to GitHub.

When you attempt to connect to GitHub, GitHub uses the public key to verify your identity based on the private key stored on your machine.

2. Generating SSH Keys

To generate SSH keys, follow these steps:

1. **Open your terminal** and run the following command to generate a new SSH key pair:

   ```css
   ssh-keygen -t rsa -b 4096 -C "your_email@example.com"
   ```

2. When prompted, choose the file where the SSH key will be saved. Press **Enter** to accept the default location (~/.ssh/id_rsa).
3. You will be asked to enter a passphrase (optional). If you choose to set one, it adds an additional layer of security.
4. Once the keys are generated, the public key is stored in the file ~/.ssh/id_rsa.pub.

3. Adding the SSH Key to GitHub

Now that you have generated your SSH key pair, you need to add the public key to your GitHub account.

1. **Copy the public key** to your clipboard:

```bash
cat ~/.ssh/id_rsa.pub
```

2. Go to GitHub, click on your profile picture, and go to **Settings**.
3. In the left sidebar, click **SSH and GPG keys**, then click **New SSH key**.
4. Paste your public key into the **Key** field, and give it a meaningful title (e.g., My Laptop SSH Key).
5. Click **Add SSH Key**.

4. Testing the SSH Connection

To ensure that the SSH key is working correctly, you can test the connection:

```css
ssh -T git@github.com
```

If successful, you'll see a message confirming that the authentication was successful.

5. Using SSH for Git Operations

Once your SSH key is set up, you can clone repositories and interact with GitHub without needing to enter your username and password each time. For example:

bash

```
git clone git@github.com:username/repository.git
```

Real-World Example: Managing Access to a Private Repository

Let's walk through a **real-world example** where we manage access to a private repository using GitHub's security features.

Scenario: You're the lead developer on a project that is hosted on GitHub, and you need to manage access to a private repository. You want to give the project's developers write access and limit access for external contributors.

Step 1: Creating a Private Repository

1. Create a new repository on GitHub and set it to **private** to restrict access to only authorized users.
2. The repository is now available only to people who are invited as collaborators or who belong to your organization.

Step 2: Adding Collaborators

1. Go to the repository's **Settings** tab and click on **Collaborators & teams**.
2. Add the developers who need write access to the repository.
3. Set their permissions to **Write** or **Admin**, depending on the level of access you want to grant them.

Step 3: Setting Up SSH Keys for Developers

Each developer needs to set up their own SSH key for accessing the repository. For instance:

- Developer Alice generates her SSH key and adds it to GitHub.
- Developer Bob does the same.
- You ensure that both Alice and Bob have access to the repository and can push changes without using passwords.

Step 4: Managing Access with Teams

1. If you are using an organization on GitHub, you can create a team (e.g., `dev-team`) and assign the repository to that team with **Write** access.
2. This way, whenever new developers join the team, they automatically get access to the repository without needing to manually add them as collaborators.

Step 5: Revoking Access

If, for example, Developer Bob leaves the project, you can go to the **Collaborators & teams** section and remove him from the repository.

Step 6: Using SSH for Secure Access

Now, both Alice and Bob can securely clone the repository and push changes without needing to enter their GitHub credentials each time.

In this chapter, we covered the key aspects of **security and access control** on GitHub, including:

- **Managing collaborators and teams**: Adding collaborators to repositories and managing access using GitHub's permission system.
- **Securing repositories with SSH keys**: Setting up SSH keys for secure, password-free access to repositories.
- A **real-world example** of managing access to a private repository by setting up collaborators and teams, and using SSH for secure communication.

By properly managing access and securing your repositories, you can ensure that your code remains protected and that the right people have the right level of access to your projects. In the next chapter, we will dive deeper into **GitHub security best practices**, such as setting up branch protection rules and managing security vulnerabilities.

Chapter 19: Git Workflow Models

In this chapter, we will explore common **Git workflow models** that help teams collaborate efficiently and maintain a clean and organized project history. We will cover the **Centralized workflow**, **Feature branching**, **GitFlow**, and **Forking workflow**, discussing how they work, their advantages, and how to choose the right one for your team. We'll also provide a **real-world example** of a startup team using the **GitFlow** model to manage their development process.

Common Git Workflows

Git workflows define the strategy and process for using Git in a collaborative development environment. Choosing the right workflow ensures that your team works efficiently and avoids conflicts while maintaining a clear and understandable project history. Let's look at the four most commonly used Git workflows:

1. Centralized Workflow

The **Centralized Workflow** is one of the simplest Git workflows and is commonly used in small teams or when working on a project with a limited number of contributors. It is based on the idea that there is one central repository where all developers commit their changes.

- **How it works**:

- All developers clone the central repository.
- Developers create feature branches locally and push their changes directly to the central repository.
- There is no complex branching strategy, and everyone works directly off the central repository.

- **Advantages**:
  - Simple to implement and understand.
  - Works well for small teams or solo developers.
- **Disadvantages**:
  - Potential for conflicts if multiple developers are working on the same files.
  - Lack of branching means features or fixes can get mixed together.
- **When to use**:
  - Ideal for small teams or solo developers where there is no need for a structured branching strategy.

2. Feature Branching

The **Feature Branching Workflow** is one of the most widely used Git workflows, especially in medium to large teams. In this workflow, developers create separate branches for each new feature or bug fix, making it easier to manage and isolate work.

- **How it works**:
  - Developers create a new branch for each feature or bug fix.

- The feature branch is typically created from the main or develop branch.
- After the work is completed, the feature branch is merged back into the main branch.

- **Advantages**:
  - Isolates work on individual features, reducing conflicts.
  - Makes it easier to organize and review code.
- **Disadvantages**:
  - Can become cumbersome with too many branches.
  - Requires discipline to manage branches and merges properly.
- **When to use**:
  - Suitable for medium to large teams, especially when working on multiple features simultaneously.

3. GitFlow

GitFlow is a more structured Git workflow that introduces dedicated branches for development, releases, and hotfixes. It was popularized by Vincent Driessen and provides a clear structure for managing releases, bug fixes, and features in parallel.

- **How it works**:
  - **Main Branches**:
    - master: This is the production-ready branch that holds the official release history.

  - develop: This is where all the ongoing development happens. New features are merged into this branch.
- **Supporting Branches**:
  - feature/<feature-name>: These branches are created from develop for new features.
  - release/<version>: When the code in develop is ready for a release, a release branch is created.
  - hotfix/<issue>: These branches are created from master for critical fixes to be quickly deployed to production.
- **Workflow**:

  0. A developer creates a feature branch from develop.
  1. Once the feature is finished, it is merged back into develop.
  2. When the develop branch is stable and ready for a release, a release branch is created from develop and merged into both master and develop.
  3. For emergency fixes, a hotfix branch is created from master, merged back into both master and develop.

- **Advantages**:

  - Well-structured and flexible for handling features, releases, and hotfixes.
  - Provides a clear separation of work for different stages of development.
- **Disadvantages**:
  - Can be overkill for small projects or teams.
  - Requires strict discipline to follow the branching model and manage merges.
- **When to use**:
  - Best for teams working on large projects with frequent releases, where stability and release management are critical.

4. Forking Workflow

The **Forking Workflow** is commonly used in open-source projects and allows external contributors to propose changes to a project without needing write access to the original repository. In this workflow, contributors fork the repository, work on their changes in their own copy, and submit pull requests.

- **How it works**:
  - Developers fork the repository (creating a personal copy of the repository).
  - They clone the forked repository to their local machine, make changes, and push the changes to their forked repository.

  - Once the changes are ready, a pull request is created from the forked repository to the original repository.
- **Advantages**:
  - External contributors can propose changes without requiring access to the original repository.
  - No need for direct write access to the main repository.
- **Disadvantages**:
  - Can slow down the workflow due to the need for pull requests and code reviews.
  - Requires proper coordination and management of pull requests.
- **When to use**:
  - Ideal for open-source projects or when working with external contributors.

Choosing the Right Workflow for Your Team

The best Git workflow for your team depends on several factors, including the size of your team, the complexity of your project, and your release cycle. Here's a quick guide to help you choose the right workflow:

- **Small Teams / Solo Developers**: The **Centralized Workflow** is often sufficient for simple projects, as it minimizes the complexity of branching and merging.

- **Medium to Large Teams**: **Feature Branching** works well for teams that need to work on multiple features simultaneously without interfering with each other's work.
- **Large Teams / Complex Projects**: **GitFlow** is a good choice when you need a structured approach to managing features, releases, and hotfixes. It's especially useful when you need to manage multiple release cycles.
- **Open-Source Projects / External Contributors**: The **Forking Workflow** is ideal for open-source projects, where contributors don't have direct access to the main repository but can propose changes via pull requests.

Real-World Example: A Startup Team Using GitFlow

Let's consider a **startup team** working on a web application. The team follows the **GitFlow** workflow because the project is growing and has multiple developers working on different features and bug fixes.

Step 1: Set Up GitFlow

The team sets up GitFlow in their repository. They have the master branch for production code, and the develop branch for ongoing development. Each new feature is developed in a separate feature/<feature-name> branch, and when the code is ready, it is merged back into develop.

Step 2: Feature Development

Developer Alice is working on a new feature to implement user authentication. She creates a new branch from develop:

```bash
git checkout -b feature/user-authentication
```

She works on the feature and commits her changes. Once the feature is ready, Alice merges it back into develop:

```sql
git checkout develop
git merge feature/user-authentication
```

Step 3: Preparing for Release

Once the develop branch is stable and contains the latest features, the team prepares for a new release. They create a release branch:

```arduino
git checkout -b release/1.0.0 develop
```

They do final testing and bug fixes in the release branch. Once everything is stable, they merge the release branch into both master (for deployment) and develop (to include any last-minute changes):

```sql
git checkout master
git merge release/1.0.0
```

```
git tag -a v1.0.0 -m "Version 1.0.0 release"
git push origin master --tags
```

Step 4: Hotfixes

A critical bug is found in the master branch, so the team creates a hotfix branch to fix the issue:

bash

```
git checkout -b hotfix/fix-login-bug master
```

They make the fix, test it, and merge the hotfix branch back into both master and develop:

bash

```
git checkout master
git merge hotfix/fix-login-bug
git checkout develop
git merge hotfix/fix-login-bug
```

In this chapter, we explored **Git workflow models**, including:

- **Centralized Workflow**: Simple and effective for small teams or solo developers.
- **Feature Branching**: Useful for medium to large teams working on multiple features simultaneously.

- **GitFlow**: A structured workflow ideal for large teams and complex projects, with clear separation between features, releases, and hotfixes.
- **Forking Workflow**: Perfect for open-source projects, where external contributors work in their own forks and submit pull requests.

We also reviewed a **real-world example** of a **startup team using GitFlow**, where they manage features, releases, and hotfixes efficiently. By adopting the appropriate Git workflow, your team can streamline collaboration and keep your project organized as it grows. In the next chapter, we will explore advanced **Git merging strategies** and how to handle merge conflicts effectively in more complex workflows.

Chapter 20: Reverting and Undoing Changes

In this chapter, we will explore how to **undo changes** in Git using commands like git revert, git reset, and git checkout. These commands provide different ways to roll back to a previous state in your Git history, whether you want to undo a commit, unstage changes, or recover files. We will also walk through a **real-world example** of fixing a mistaken commit or merge to illustrate how to use these tools effectively.

Using git revert, git reset, and git checkout to Undo Changes

There are several ways to undo changes in Git, depending on the type of change you want to undo and the current state of your repository. Let's dive into each of these commands and explore how they work.

1. git revert

The git revert command is used to **create a new commit** that undoes the changes introduced by a previous commit. Unlike git reset, which alters the commit history, git revert preserves the history and creates a new commit that effectively undoes the previous commit's changes.

- **When to use**: Use git revert when you need to undo a commit but still want to maintain a clear, intact commit history. This is commonly used in shared repositories or when working in a collaborative environment, as it doesn't rewrite history.
- **How to use**:

php

```
git revert <commit-hash>
```

This will create a new commit that undoes the changes introduced by the specified commit.

For example, to undo the last commit:

```
git revert HEAD
```

Git will open your default text editor to allow you to write a commit message for the revert commit. Once you save and close the editor, the revert commit is created.

2. git reset

The git reset command is used to **reset the current branch to a previous commit**. There are three main types of resets: **soft**, **mixed**, and **hard**. Each reset type affects the working directory and staging area differently.

- **Soft reset**: Resets the commit history but leaves the changes staged.

```css
git reset --soft <commit-hash>
```

Use this if you want to move the HEAD pointer to a previous commit but keep all changes in the staging area, so you can recommit them.

- **Mixed reset** (default): Resets the commit history and unstages the changes but keeps them in the working directory.

```perl
git reset <commit-hash>
```

This is useful if you want to unstage changes after committing, but keep the changes in your working directory for further edits.

- **Hard reset**: Resets the commit history, staging area, and working directory to the specified commit, discarding any changes.

```css
git reset --hard <commit-hash>
```

This will **lose all local changes** that have not been committed, so use it with caution. It's often used when you want to completely discard changes and revert to a clean state.

3. git checkout

The git checkout command is typically used to **switch branches** or **restore files** in your working directory to a previous state.

- **When to use**: You can use git checkout to undo changes in specific files, or when you want to checkout a different branch or commit without affecting the rest of your working directory.
- **How to use**:
    - To discard changes in a file and restore it to the last committed version:

      ```lua
      git checkout -- <file>
      ```

    - To switch to a different branch:

      ```php
      git checkout <branch-name>
      ```

    - To restore a file to a specific commit version:

      php

```
git checkout <commit-hash> -- <file>
```

Comparison of git revert, git reset, and git checkout

Command	Action	Use Case
git revert	Creates a new commit that undoes a previous commit	Undo a commit without rewriting history
git reset	Moves the HEAD to a previous commit and optionally modifies the working directory/staging area	Undo commits, unstage changes, or reset to a clean state
git checkout	Switch branches or restore files to a specific commit state	Undo changes to files or switch to a different branch/commit

---

How to Roll Back to a Previous State

In Git, "rolling back" typically means returning to a previous commit, either by **undoing a commit** or **restoring files**. The method you choose depends on your needs:

1. Using git revert to Undo a Commit

Let's say you made a commit that introduced a bug or a feature that should not have been merged into the codebase. Instead of resetting the commit history, you can use git revert to undo it.

- Example: You mistakenly committed code that introduced an error. To undo it without rewriting history:

  php

  ```
  git revert <commit-hash>
  ```

This creates a new commit that undoes the changes introduced by the previous commit. You can then push the revert commit to the remote repository.

2. Using git reset to Roll Back to a Specific Commit

If you want to **remove commits** entirely and reset your branch to a specific point, git reset is the way to go.

- **Soft reset**: Move the HEAD pointer to a previous commit while keeping changes staged:

  css

  ```
  git reset --soft <commit-hash>
  ```

- **Mixed reset**: Move the HEAD pointer to a previous commit and unstage the changes:

  perl

```
git reset <commit-hash>
```

- **Hard reset**: Reset the repository completely to a previous commit, discarding all changes:

```css
git reset --hard <commit-hash>
```

3. Using git checkout to Restore Files

If you only need to discard changes to specific files, use `git checkout`:

- Example: You're working on a file but decide to discard the changes and return it to its last committed state:

```lua
git checkout -- <file>
```

If you want to reset a file to its state at a previous commit:

```php
git checkout <commit-hash> -- <file>
```

Real-World Example: Fixing a Mistaken Commit or Merge

Let's walk through a **real-world example** where you accidentally committed or merged changes that introduced issues, and you need to fix it.

Scenario: A developer mistakenly merged a feature branch into main, but the feature isn't ready yet and contains incomplete or buggy code. The team wants to roll back the merge without losing any other work done on main.

Step 1: Identifying the Problematic Merge Commit

After realizing that the merge was a mistake, you need to identify the commit where the merge occurred. You can use git log to find the commit hash of the merge:

bash

```
git log
```

Find the merge commit, which typically has a message like "Merge branch 'feature-xyz' into main".

Step 2: Reverting the Merge Commit

To undo the merge without rewriting history, you can use git revert:

sql

```
git revert -m 1 <merge-commit-hash>
```

The -m 1 flag specifies that you want to revert to the main branch's version before the merge (i.e., the first parent of the merge). This creates a new commit that undoes the changes introduced by the merge.

Step 3: Pushing the Revert Commit

After reverting the merge, you can push the changes to the remote repository:

```css
git push origin main
```

Step 4: Restoring the Feature Branch (Optional)

If the feature branch still needs to be worked on, you can leave it as is, or you can create a new branch from main to continue work on the feature.

- Example: To continue working on the feature, create a new branch from main:

  ```bash
  git checkout -b feature/xyz-fix
  ```

In this chapter, we discussed various ways to **undo changes** in Git, including using:

- **git revert** to create a new commit that undoes changes from a previous commit.
- **git reset** to move the HEAD pointer and reset the staging area and working directory.

- **git checkout** to restore files to a previous state or switch to another branch.

We also walked through a **real-world example** of undoing a mistaken merge using git revert and how to fix a problematic commit or merge without rewriting the project history. Understanding these commands gives you powerful tools to maintain a clean and efficient Git workflow, even when mistakes happen. In the next chapter, we will discuss **Git best practices** for collaboration and version control in team environments.

Chapter 21: Optimizing Your Git Workflow

In this chapter, we will explore several ways to **optimize your Git workflow**, making your development process faster, more efficient, and easier to manage. We'll cover how to **speed up your workflow with Git aliases and hooks**, provide **performance tips for large repositories**, and offer a **real-world example** of optimizing a large codebase for better efficiency.

Speeding Up Your Workflow with Git Aliases and Hooks

Git provides powerful tools like **aliases** and **hooks** to automate repetitive tasks, saving time and reducing errors. Let's dive into these two concepts and how they can enhance your workflow.

1. Git Aliases

Git aliases are custom shortcuts for commonly used Git commands. They allow you to define shorter, easier-to-type commands that perform the same functions as the original Git commands.

- **How to Create Aliases**: You can define Git aliases in your global Git configuration file (~/.gitconfig). To create an alias, use the following command:

  csharp

git config --global alias.<alias-name> '<command>'

- **Examples of Useful Aliases**:
    - Shorten git status to git st:

      csharp

      ```
      git config --global alias.st status
      ```

    - Shorten git commit -m to git cm:

      csharp

      ```
      git config --global alias.cm "commit -m"
      ```

    - View a more concise log with one-line commit summaries:

      css

      ```
      git config --global alias.lg "log --oneline --graph --decorate --all"
      ```

- After defining these aliases, you can run:
    - git st instead of git status.
    - git cm "message" instead of git commit -m "message".
    - git lg to view a graphical, simplified log.
- **Why Use Aliases**:

- They make your commands faster to type and easier to remember.
- They help reduce the chance of typos or mistakes in frequently used commands.

2. Git Hooks

Git hooks are scripts that run automatically when certain events occur in a Git repository. They allow you to automate tasks such as code formatting, linting, testing, or deploying code whenever a specific Git operation is executed.

- **Types of Hooks**: Git supports a wide range of hooks, including:
  - **pre-commit**: Runs before a commit is made. You can use it to run tests or format code before committing.
  - **post-commit**: Runs after a commit is made, ideal for logging or notifications.
  - **pre-push**: Runs before pushing changes to the remote repository.
  - **post-merge**: Runs after a merge is completed.
- **How to Set Up Git Hooks**: Git hooks are stored in the .git/hooks/ directory within your repository. You can add custom scripts here to automate tasks.

For example, to run tests before every commit, you can set up a pre-commit hook:

0. Navigate to .git/hooks/ and open the pre-commit.sample file.
    1. Rename it to pre-commit (without the .sample).
    2. Add your script (for example, running tests):

```bash
#!/bin/sh
npm test
if [ $? -ne 0 ]; then
  echo "Tests failed. Commit aborted."
  exit 1
fi
```

This will run npm test before each commit. If the tests fail, the commit is aborted.

- **Why Use Git Hooks**:
    - Automate tasks and ensure code quality.
    - Prevent mistakes (like committing code with failing tests or improper formatting).
    - Save time by reducing the need to manually run certain operations.

Performance Tips for Large Repositories

When working with **large repositories** or **monolithic codebases**, Git can sometimes become slow or inefficient, especially as the number of commits, branches, or files grows. Here are some tips to improve performance and speed up your workflow when working with large repositories.

1. Avoid Storing Large Files in Git

Git is designed to track changes to text-based files efficiently, but it struggles with large binary files (like images, videos, or compiled assets). Storing large binary files directly in your Git repository can slow down performance, especially when cloning or fetching from the repository.

- **Solution: Use Git LFS (Large File Storage)**: Git LFS replaces large files with lightweight references in your repository, while storing the actual content in a separate location.

  To use Git LFS:

  1. Install Git LFS:

     ```
     git lfs install
     ```

  2. Track the file types you want to store with LFS:

     ```
     arduino
     ```

```
git lfs track "*.mp4"
```

This helps keep your repository small and improves performance when working with large files.

2. Clean Up Old Branches and Tags

Over time, your repository may accumulate old branches and tags that are no longer needed, which can slow down Git operations.

- **Solution: Delete Old Branches and Tags**:
  - Delete local branches that have been merged:

    ```php
    git branch -d <branch-name>
    ```

  - Delete remote branches:

    ```perl
    git push origin --delete <branch-name>
    ```

  - Delete tags:

    ```perl
    git tag -d <tag-name>
    git push --delete origin <tag-name>
    ```

- Regularly cleaning up your repository ensures that Git can operate efficiently and reduces clutter.

3. Use Shallow Clones

When cloning large repositories, a shallow clone can be useful if you don't need the full commit history.

- **Solution: Clone Only the Latest Commit History**:

  bash

  ```
  git clone --depth 1 <repository-url>
  ```

  This creates a clone with only the most recent commit, saving time and disk space.

4. Optimize Git's Internal Database

Git uses a database to store all its internal objects. Over time, this database can become fragmented, which may affect performance.

- **Solution: Run Git's Garbage Collection**:

  css

  ```
  git gc --aggressive
  ```

  This command cleans up unnecessary files and optimizes the internal structure of the repository, improving performance.

Real-World Example: Optimizing a Large Codebase

Let's consider a **real-world example** of a large project where the development team is working on a monolithic codebase, and they need to optimize their Git workflow.

Scenario: A development team is working on a large web application with thousands of commits, multiple feature branches, and large media assets. The team experiences slow performance when cloning the repository, checking out branches, or fetching updates.

Step 1: Using Git LFS for Large Files

The repository contains large image and video files that were slowing down Git operations. The team decides to use Git LFS to store these files more efficiently.

1. Install Git LFS and configure it to track large files:

   ```
   bash

   git lfs install
   git lfs track "*.jpg" "*.mp4"
   ```

2. After configuring LFS, the team migrates existing large files to Git LFS, reducing the repository size and improving Git performance.

Step 2: Deleting Old Branches

The repository has accumulated many old feature branches that are no longer needed.

1. The team deletes merged branches locally:

```bash
git branch -d feature/old-feature
```

2. They also clean up old branches remotely:

```bash
git push origin --delete feature/old-feature
```

This reduces the number of references in the repository and improves performance.

Step 3: Shallow Cloning for New Developers

New developers joining the project need to clone the repository but don't require the full commit history.

1. The team recommends using a shallow clone:

```bash
git clone --depth 1 https://github.com/organization/large-project.git
```

This helps new developers get started quickly with a minimal repository size.

Step 4: Running Git Garbage Collection

The team periodically runs garbage collection to optimize Git's internal database:

1. The team runs:

```bash
git gc --aggressive
```

This improves the speed of Git operations by cleaning up unnecessary objects in the repository.

In this chapter, we explored several ways to **optimize your Git workflow**, including:

- **Git Aliases**: Creating custom shortcuts for frequently used Git commands to speed up your workflow.
- **Git Hooks**: Automating tasks like tests and code formatting to ensure consistent code quality.
- **Performance Tips for Large Repositories**: Using Git LFS to handle large files, cleaning up old branches, and optimizing the Git database for faster operations.
- **Real-World Example**: Optimizing a large codebase by implementing Git LFS, cleaning up branches, using shallow clones, and running garbage collection.

By adopting these optimizations, you can significantly improve your Git workflow, making it more efficient and suitable for large or complex projects. In the next chapter, we will explore **Git best practices** for collaboration and how to streamline your team's development process.

Chapter 22: Working with Submodules

In this chapter, we will dive into **Git submodules**, a powerful feature of Git that allows you to manage external repositories within your own project. This is especially useful when you want to include third-party libraries, dependencies, or shared code in your project without directly copying the code into your repository. We will cover how **Git submodules** work, how to **add** and **update** submodules, and provide a **real-world example** of managing third-party libraries in a project.

What Are Git Submodules and How Do They Work?

A **Git submodule** is essentially a Git repository embedded inside another Git repository. Submodules allow you to include one Git repository as a subdirectory of another repository, and Git tracks the submodule as a reference to a specific commit from the external repository. This enables you to manage dependencies, libraries, or other projects separately while still integrating them into your main project.

How Submodules Work

- A submodule is a reference to an external Git repository, stored in your main repository as a special type of Git directory.

- Submodules have their own version history and commits, independent of the main repository.
- Git keeps track of the specific commit of the submodule in your main repository, ensuring that the correct version of the submodule is used.

When you clone a repository that contains submodules, you need to initialize and update the submodules separately to pull their content.

Adding and Updating Submodules

Git provides commands to add, update, and manage submodules within a repository.

1. Adding a Submodule

To add a submodule, you need to specify the URL of the external repository and the directory where you want it to reside in your project. Here's how to do it:

1. Navigate to the root of your Git repository.
2. Run the following command to add the submodule:

   ```bash
   git submodule add <repository-url> <path-to-submodule>
   ```

   - <repository-url>: The URL of the external Git repository you want to add.

- <path-to-submodule>: The directory in your repository where the submodule should be placed.

Example:

bash

```
git submodule add https://github.com/username/third-party-library.git libs/third-party-library
```

3. After running the command, Git will:
    - Clone the submodule repository into the specified directory.
    - Add a .gitmodules file that contains the configuration for the submodule (e.g., URL, path).
    - Stage the .gitmodules file and the submodule directory for commit.
4. Commit the changes:

bash

```
git commit -m "Add third-party-library as a submodule"
```

2. Cloning a Repository with Submodules

If you clone a repository that contains submodules, Git does not automatically initialize and update the submodules. You need to initialize and update the submodules manually after cloning the main repository.

1. Clone the repository:

```bash
git clone <repository-url>
```

2. After cloning, initialize the submodules:

```bash
git submodule init
```

3. Update the submodules to fetch their content:

```bash
git submodule update
```

Alternatively, you can clone the repository and initialize/update all submodules in one command:

```bash
git clone --recurse-submodules <repository-url>
```

3. Updating a Submodule

To update a submodule to the latest commit from the external repository, you need to navigate to the submodule directory and fetch the latest changes from its remote repository.

1. First, go to the submodule directory:

```bash
cd <path-to-submodule>
```

2. Then, fetch and merge the latest changes:

```bash
git fetch
git merge origin/master
```

3. After updating the submodule, return to the root directory of the main repository, stage the changes, and commit:

```bash
cd ..
git add <path-to-submodule>
git commit -m "Update third-party-library to latest commit"
```

4. Removing a Submodule

To remove a submodule from your repository:

1. Remove the submodule entry from the .gitmodules file:

```bash
git submodule deinit -f <path-to-submodule>
```

2. Remove the submodule directory:

bash

```
git rm -f <path-to-submodule>
```

3. Commit the changes:

bash

```
git commit -m "Remove third-party-library submodule"
```

4. Delete the submodule's directory and configuration:

bash

```
rm -rf .git/modules/<path-to-submodule>
```

Real-World Example: Managing Third-Party Libraries in a Project

Let's walk through a **real-world example** where a team is working on a web application, and they want to include a third-party library as a submodule.

Scenario: A development team is building a web application, and they want to include a third-party JavaScript library (e.g., a charting library) as a submodule in their project. This allows them to easily manage the library as an independent Git repository while keeping it integrated with their application.

Step 1: Adding the Third-Party Library as a Submodule

1. Navigate to the root of your project and add the third-party library as a submodule:

   bash

   ```
   git submodule add https://github.com/username/charting-library.git libs/charting-library
   ```

2. This command clones the charting-library repository into the libs/charting-library directory within your project.
3. Commit the change to your repository:

   bash

   ```
   git commit -m "Add charting-library as a submodule"
   ```

Step 2: Cloning the Project with the Submodule

New developers or team members need to clone the repository and initialize the submodule:

1. Clone the repository with the submodule:

   bash

   ```
   git clone --recurse-submodules https://github.com/organization/project.git
   ```

   Alternatively, if the repository has already been cloned:

   bash

```
git submodule init
git submodule update
```

Step 3: Updating the Submodule

As the third-party library is updated (perhaps new features or bug fixes are released), the team needs to pull the latest changes into their project.

1. Navigate to the submodule directory:

   bash

   ```
   cd libs/charting-library
   ```

2. Fetch and merge the latest changes from the submodule repository:

   bash

   ```
   git fetch
   git merge origin/master
   ```

3. Return to the main project directory, stage, and commit the update:

   bash

   ```
   cd ../..
   git add libs/charting-library
   git commit -m "Update charting-library to the latest version"
   ```

Step 4: Removing the Submodule

If the team decides to stop using the third-party library, they can remove the submodule.

1. Deinitialize the submodule:

    bash

    ```
    git submodule deinit -f libs/charting-library
    ```

2. Remove the submodule directory:

    bash

    ```
    git rm -f libs/charting-library
    ```

3. Commit the changes:

    bash

    ```
    git commit -m "Remove charting-library submodule"
    ```

4. Clean up the submodule configuration:

    bash

    ```
    rm -rf .git/modules/libs/charting-library
    ```

In this chapter, we explored **Git submodules**, a powerful way to manage external repositories within your project. We covered:

- **What Git submodules are** and how they allow you to include other Git repositories as part of your project.
- **How to add and update submodules** using commands like git submodule add, git submodule update, and git submodule init.
- **Real-world example** of managing third-party libraries using Git submodules, showing how to add, update, and remove submodules in your project.

Git submodules are essential for managing dependencies, shared code, or external libraries in a clean and efficient way. In the next chapter, we will explore how to handle **merge conflicts** and strategies for resolving them during collaborative development.

Chapter 23: GitHub for Open-Source Contributions

In this chapter, we will explore how to contribute to open-source projects using GitHub, which has become the central hub for collaboration in open-source development. We'll cover how to **contribute to open-source projects**, the process of **forking** repositories, **submitting pull requests**, and **working with maintainers**. We will also walk through a **real-world example** of a developer contributing to an open-source project to demonstrate the process from start to finish.

How to Contribute to Open-Source Projects

Contributing to open-source projects is a great way to give back to the community, improve your skills, and collaborate with other developers. Here's a general overview of how to contribute:

1. **Find a Project to Contribute To**: You can find open-source projects on GitHub by browsing repositories or searching for topics of interest. GitHub has a feature called **GitHub Explore** that helps you discover popular projects based on your interests. Additionally, many repositories have tags like good first issue or help wanted to indicate beginner-friendly or urgent tasks.

2. **Fork the Repository**: In open-source contributions, you don't directly push to the main repository. Instead, you **fork** the repository to create a personal copy of the project. You make changes to this forked repository and then submit those changes through a **pull request**.
3. **Clone Your Fork**: After forking a repository, you clone your fork to your local machine to begin working on it. This is the version of the repository you will make changes to.
4. **Make Your Changes**: Once you have cloned the repository, you can start making your changes, whether it's fixing a bug, adding a feature, or improving documentation.
5. **Submit a Pull Request**: After making changes, you push them to your fork and create a **pull request** to propose your changes to the original project. The project maintainers will review your changes and may ask for revisions before merging your pull request.

Forking, Submitting Pull Requests, and Working with Maintainers

Now that we've covered the basic steps, let's look at the specifics of the key actions involved in contributing to an open-source project: **forking, submitting pull requests**, and **working with maintainers**.

1. Forking a Repository

Forking a repository creates a personal copy of the repository under your GitHub account. You can make changes freely in your fork without affecting the original project.

1. **Go to the Repository**: Navigate to the repository you want to contribute to on GitHub.
2. **Click Fork**: In the top right corner of the repository page, click the **Fork** button. This creates a copy of the repository in your GitHub account.

Once you have forked the repository, you can clone it to your local machine:

bash

```
git clone https://github.com/your-username/repository-name.git
```

2. Submitting a Pull Request

After making changes to your fork, you'll want to propose your changes to the original repository. This is done by creating a **pull request (PR)**. A PR allows the repository maintainers to review your changes before they are merged into the main project.

1. **Push Your Changes**: Once you've made your changes and committed them, push them to your fork:

   perl

   ```
   git push origin branch-name
   ```

2. **Open a Pull Request**: Go to the original repository on GitHub, and you will typically see a banner that prompts you to **Compare & pull request** once you've pushed your changes. Click on it.
3. **Describe Your Changes**: Provide a clear and concise description of what changes you've made, why they are necessary, and if they solve any existing issues. It's also helpful to link to the issue number if the pull request addresses a specific problem (e.g., Fixes #45).
4. **Submit the Pull Request**: Once you've written a good description and reviewed your changes, click **Create pull request**.

3. Working with Maintainers

After submitting a pull request, the project maintainers will review it. They may:

- **Request Changes**: If there are any issues with your code, the maintainers will ask you to make changes. You can update your pull request by pushing additional commits to your branch.
- **Merge the Pull Request**: If the changes are approved, the maintainers will merge your pull request into the main repository.

Here are a few best practices for working with maintainers:

- **Be Patient**: Open-source maintainers are often volunteers and may take some time to review pull requests.
- **Respond to Feedback**: If maintainers request changes, respond promptly and make the necessary adjustments.
- **Be Respectful**: Maintain a professional and courteous tone when communicating with maintainers and other contributors.

Real-World Example: A Developer Contributing to an Open-Source Project

Let's walk through a **real-world example** of a developer, Alex, contributing to an open-source project.

Scenario: Alex is a developer who is interested in contributing to an open-source project called AwesomeProject, which is a library for managing tasks in JavaScript. Alex notices a bug in the task sorting feature and decides to submit a fix.

Step 1: Forking the Repository

1. Alex finds the project on GitHub by searching for AwesomeProject.
2. On the project's GitHub page, Alex clicks the **Fork** button to create a personal copy of the repository in their account.

Step 2: Cloning the Forked Repository

Alex clones the forked repository to their local machine:

```bash
git clone https://github.com/alex123/AwesomeProject.git
cd AwesomeProject
```

Step 3: Creating a Branch for the Fix

Alex creates a new branch for the bug fix:

```css
git checkout -b fix-sort-bug
```

Step 4: Making the Changes

Alex identifies the issue with the sorting algorithm in the JavaScript code. After fixing the bug, they run tests to ensure the fix works.

Step 5: Committing and Pushing the Changes

After testing the fix, Alex commits the changes:

```perl
git add .
git commit -m "Fix bug in task sorting algorithm"
git push origin fix-sort-bug
```

Step 6: Creating a Pull Request

Alex goes to the original AwesomeProject repository on GitHub and clicks the **Compare & pull request** button. In the description, they explain:

- What the bug was.
- How their fix addresses the problem.
- Mention that they ran the test suite and it passed.

The pull request is created.

Step 7: Working with Maintainers

The maintainer of AwesomeProject, Taylor, reviews the pull request. They suggest some changes to improve the efficiency of the fix. Alex makes the suggested changes and pushes them to the same branch:

lua

```
git commit --amend
git push origin fix-sort-bug --force
```

Taylor reviews the updated changes and merges the pull request into the main project.

Step 8: Closing the Loop

Once the pull request is merged, Alex's contribution is part of AwesomeProject. They thank Taylor for reviewing the pull request and continue to monitor the project for any further contributions they can make.

In this chapter, we covered the process of contributing to **open-source projects** on GitHub, including:

- **Forking a repository** to create a personal copy and working on changes locally.
- **Submitting a pull request (PR)** to propose changes to the original project.
- **Working with maintainers** by responding to feedback and making necessary changes.

We also walked through a **real-world example** of a developer contributing to an open-source project by fixing a bug and submitting a pull request. This example highlighted the importance of clear communication, collaboration, and patience when contributing to open-source projects.

Contributing to open-source not only helps improve projects that you rely on but also allows you to learn, connect with other developers, and enhance your skills. In the next chapter, we will explore **advanced Git features** for handling complex workflows and large-scale repositories.

Chapter 24: Troubleshooting Git Issues

In this chapter, we will explore common **Git errors** that developers frequently encounter and provide solutions for resolving them. We will also cover how to debug and solve issues related to **failed merges, pull requests**, and **authentication errors**. Finally, we'll walk through a **real-world example** of resolving a merge conflict in a large team scenario, which is one of the most common challenges in collaborative development.

Common Git Errors and How to Solve Them

Git, like any tool, can throw errors. Understanding how to resolve common Git errors will help you avoid disruptions and keep your development workflow running smoothly.

1. Merge Conflicts

A **merge conflict** occurs when Git cannot automatically reconcile differences between two branches. This usually happens when changes are made to the same line in a file or when a file is deleted in one branch and modified in the other.

- **How to Resolve**:
    1. Git will mark the file as conflicted and highlight the conflicting sections within the file. Conflicts are typically surrounded by markers like:

markdown

```
<<<<<<< HEAD
changes from the current branch
=======
changes from the branch you're merging
>>>>>>> branch-name
```

2. Manually edit the file to resolve the conflict, choosing which changes to keep.
3. After resolving the conflicts, stage the changes:

csharp

```
git add <conflicted-file>
```

4. Finally, commit the resolution:

sql

```
git commit
```

2. Authentication Errors

Authentication errors occur when Git cannot verify your identity when interacting with remote repositories. This is commonly seen with HTTPS or SSH connections.

- **Common Errors**:
  - **HTTPS**: fatal: Authentication failed
  - **SSH**: Permission denied (publickey)

- **How to Solve**:
  - For **HTTPS authentication errors**, ensure your Git credentials are correct. If you've changed your password, use the new credentials, or consider using a Git credential manager to securely store your credentials.
    - You can also use **personal access tokens** if GitHub requires them instead of your GitHub password.
  - For **SSH authentication errors**, ensure your SSH key is correctly set up and added to GitHub. Check if your key is registered with GitHub by running:

    css

    ```
    ssh -T git@github.com
    ```

    If necessary, regenerate your SSH keys and add them to GitHub under **Settings > SSH and GPG keys**.

3. Detached HEAD State

A **detached HEAD** occurs when you check out a commit rather than a branch. In this state, any changes you make won't be associated with a branch, and you may lose your work if you don't create a new branch.

- **How to Solve**:

1. If you're in a detached HEAD state and you want to keep your changes, create a new branch to track them:

```arduino
git checkout -b new-branch
```

2. If you want to go back to the original branch, use:

```css
git checkout main
```

4. Merge Commit Not Fast-Forwarded

A **non-fast-forward error** happens when you try to push your changes but the remote branch has new commits that your local branch doesn't have.

- **How to Solve**:
  1. First, pull the latest changes from the remote repository:

     ```css
     git pull origin main
     ```

  2. Resolve any conflicts if they appear.
  3. Once your local branch is up to date, push your changes:

```css
git push origin main
```

5. Rebase Conflicts

If you encounter conflicts during a rebase, Git will stop and ask you to resolve the conflicts before continuing. The process is similar to resolving conflicts during a merge.

- **How to Solve**:
  1. Resolve the conflicts in the same way as you would during a merge.
  2. Once resolved, continue the rebase:

     ```kotlin
     git rebase --continue
     ```

  3. If you decide that the rebase is too complicated or problematic, you can abort it:

     ```c
     git rebase --abort
     ```

Debugging Failed Merges, Pull Requests, and Authentication Errors

Sometimes merges, pull requests, or authentication fail due to various issues. Here's how to debug and solve these problems:

1. Debugging Failed Merges

A failed merge usually results from conflicting changes in the same lines of code or files being deleted or modified in both branches. Follow these steps to debug:

1. **Check for Conflicts**: Use `git status` to identify conflicted files.
2. **Inspect Conflicted Files**: Open each conflicted file and manually resolve conflicts.
3. **Stage the Changes**: After resolving conflicts, stage the files:

   csharp

   ```
   git add <conflicted-file>
   ```

4. **Commit the Merge**: Once all conflicts are resolved, commit the merge:

   sql

   ```
   git commit
   ```

2. Debugging Failed Pull Requests

Pull requests can fail for several reasons:

- **Out-of-date base branch**: If the base branch (e.g., main) has moved forward, you might need to merge or rebase the changes.
- **Merge conflicts**: Ensure there are no conflicts in the files being merged.

How to Fix:

1. Update your feature branch by merging or rebasing:

   ```sql
   git fetch origin
   git merge origin/main
   ```

2. Resolve any conflicts and push the changes to your pull request branch:

   ```perl
   git push origin feature-branch
   ```

3. Debugging Authentication Errors

Authentication errors occur when Git cannot verify your identity with the remote repository.

How to Solve:

1. **Check your credentials**: Ensure your username and password (or personal access token for GitHub) are correct.
2. **Use SSH**: If you're using HTTPS for authentication and facing issues, switch to SSH to bypass credential prompts. Set up an SSH key and add it to GitHub.
3. **Credential Manager**: For HTTPS authentication, use Git's credential manager to securely store your credentials:

   lua

   ```
   git config --global credential.helper manager
   ```

Real-World Example: Resolving a Merge Conflict in a Large Team

Let's consider a **real-world scenario** where a large development team is working on a shared project, and two developers (Alice and Bob) encounter a merge conflict.

Scenario: Alice is working on implementing a new feature in the feature/login branch, while Bob is working on fixing bugs in the bugfix/navbar branch. Both Alice and Bob modify the same lines in the index.html file, leading to a conflict when they try to merge their branches into main.

Step 1: Alice's Commit

1. Alice finishes her feature and commits her changes:

```bash
git add index.html
git commit -m "Add login form"
```

2. Alice pushes her changes to the remote feature/login branch:

```bash
git push origin feature/login
```

Step 2: Bob's Commit

1. Meanwhile, Bob also finishes his bug fixes and commits:

```bash
git add index.html
git commit -m "Fix navbar bug"
```

2. Bob pushes his changes to the remote bugfix/navbar branch:

```bash
git push origin bugfix/navbar
```

Step 3: Merge Conflict

When Alice tries to merge her feature/login branch into main, she gets a merge conflict because both she and Bob modified the same lines in the index.html file.

- Alice checks for merge conflicts using:

```bash
git merge origin/main
```

- Git flags index.html as conflicted.

Step 4: Resolving the Conflict

Alice opens the index.html file, where Git has marked the conflicting sections:

```html
<<<<<<< HEAD
<!-- Alice's changes (login form) -->
=======
<!-- Bob's changes (navbar bug fix) -->
>>>>>>> feature/login
```

Alice manually resolves the conflict by combining both the login form and navbar fix, and then stages the changes:

```bash
git add index.html
```

Step 5: Completing the Merge

Once the conflict is resolved and staged, Alice commits the merge:

bash

```
git commit -m "Resolve merge conflict between login feature and navbar fix"
```

Finally, Alice pushes the changes to the remote main branch:

```bash
git push origin main
```

Now, the merge conflict is resolved, and both Alice and Bob's changes are successfully integrated into the main branch.

In this chapter, we covered:

- Common **Git errors** like merge conflicts, authentication errors, and detached HEAD states, and how to solve them.
- How to **debug failed merges**, pull requests, and authentication errors.
- A **real-world example** of resolving a merge conflict in a large team scenario, demonstrating how to handle conflicts and collaborate effectively.

Troubleshooting Git issues is an essential skill that ensures your development workflow remains smooth and efficient. In the next chapter, we will discuss **Git best practices** for managing large teams, including branching strategies, commit conventions, and workflow optimizations.

Chapter 25: Mastering Git and GitHub for Team Collaboration

In this chapter, we will explore best practices for **working in teams with Git and GitHub** to ensure smooth collaboration and effective version control. We'll cover **how to scale GitHub workflows** in large teams and demonstrate how to manage a multi-developer project with complex workflows. This chapter will provide insights into optimizing Git and GitHub usage in team environments, which is critical for maintaining a clean and efficient project history as the team grows.

Best Practices for Working in Teams with Git and GitHub

Collaborating on Git and GitHub is an essential part of modern software development. Here are some best practices that will help teams work together more effectively and avoid common pitfalls.

1. Use a Consistent Branching Strategy

A consistent **branching strategy** is vital for keeping the development process organized, especially as the team grows. Popular branching models include:

- **GitFlow**: A structured model with main, develop, and feature branches. GitFlow helps manage development, releases, and hotfixes separately.

- **Feature Branching**: Each feature or bug fix is developed in its own branch, typically from main or develop. Once the work is done, the feature branch is merged back into the main branch.
- **GitHub Flow**: A simpler branching model used by teams that deploy continuously. Developers create a new branch from main for each task and merge it back once the task is completed and tested.

2. Commit Frequently and with Clear Messages

- **Commit Often**: Small, frequent commits make it easier to track changes, resolve conflicts, and understand the history. Aim to commit logical chunks of work rather than large, monolithic changes.
- **Clear Commit Messages**: Use meaningful commit messages that explain the reason for the change. Follow a consistent format (e.g., **feat** for new features, **fix** for bug fixes) and keep the messages concise but descriptive.

  Example of a good commit message:

  scss

  ```
  feat(auth): Implement JWT authentication for login
  ```

3. Use Pull Requests for Code Review

Pull requests (PRs) are essential for code review and collaboration:

- **Code Review**: Before merging changes into the main branch, use pull requests to allow team members to review the code. This ensures code quality, reduces bugs, and improves team collaboration.
- **CI/CD Integration**: Automate testing using GitHub Actions or other CI/CD tools to run tests on every pull request, ensuring that code is tested before it is merged.
- **Provide Meaningful Descriptions**: Include a clear description of what the PR does, why the changes are necessary, and any relevant issue numbers. This helps reviewers understand the context and purpose of the changes.

4. Handle Merge Conflicts Proactively

Merge conflicts are inevitable, especially when multiple developers are working on the same files. Here are strategies to handle them:

- **Communicate with the Team**: If you anticipate conflicts, discuss with your team early on to minimize overlaps.
- **Rebase Regularly**: Regularly rebase your feature branch on the latest `develop` or `main` branch to minimize the risk of conflicts.
- **Resolve Conflicts Immediately**: When conflicts arise, resolve them quickly to avoid blocking the workflow.

5. Use Tags and Releases for Versioning

For projects that involve multiple releases, Git tags are critical for version control. You can tag a commit to mark a version or release point.

- **Tagging Releases**: Use annotated tags to mark stable releases.
- **Semantic Versioning**: Follow a consistent versioning strategy, such as semantic versioning (v1.0.0), to help team members and users understand the changes between releases.

6. Protect Important Branches

Protect critical branches like main or develop by setting branch protection rules on GitHub. This ensures that only approved commits are merged into these branches.

- **Require PRs for Merging**: Enforce pull requests for merging to prevent direct pushes.
- **Enforce CI/CD Checks**: Require that all tests pass before merging.

How to Scale GitHub Workflows in Large Teams

As your team grows, scaling workflows effectively becomes essential to maintaining efficiency and collaboration. Here are some key strategies for managing workflows in large teams:

1. Use GitHub Organizations and Teams

In large projects, managing access and permissions can become complicated. GitHub provides **Organizations** and **Teams** to handle this.

- **Create Organizations**: An organization allows you to group multiple repositories under a single account. This simplifies management for large teams.
- **Manage Teams**: Within an organization, you can create **teams** (e.g., Dev, QA, Design) and assign specific repositories and permissions to each team. This ensures that the right people have the right level of access.

2. Implement CI/CD with GitHub Actions

Scaling your CI/CD pipeline is crucial for large teams, especially when integrating code from multiple developers.

- **Automate Testing**: Use **GitHub Actions** to automatically run tests, linting, and builds on every pull request. This reduces the risk of introducing errors into the main branch.
- **Deploy Automatically**: Set up GitHub Actions to automatically deploy code to staging or production environments after a successful merge.
- **Separate Jobs for Different Environments**: Use jobs and workflows to separate builds and tests for different environments (e.g., development, staging, production).

3. Use Issue Templates and Project Boards

GitHub provides tools to help teams stay organized:

- **Issue Templates**: Set up **issue templates** for bug reports, feature requests, and tasks. This ensures that all contributors follow a consistent format when reporting issues or requesting features.
- **Project Boards**: Use **GitHub Projects** (Kanban-style boards) to organize tasks and track progress. This allows team members to visualize what needs to be done and manage workflows effectively.

4. Automate Code Reviews

In larger teams, manual code review can become a bottleneck. Automate parts of the process using GitHub Actions or third-party tools:

- **Automated Code Review**: Set up tools like **SonarCloud**, **CodeClimate**, or **Dependabot** to automatically analyze code quality, security, and dependency updates.
- **Require Approvals**: Configure your repository settings to require code review approvals before merging pull requests.

5. Use Dependency Management

In large projects, managing dependencies effectively is key:

- **Git Submodules**: If your project uses third-party code or shared libraries, consider using **Git submodules** to manage external dependencies.
- **Dependabot**: Use **Dependabot** to automatically check for outdated dependencies and create pull requests to update them.

Real-World Example: Managing a Multi-Developer Project with Complex Workflows

Let's look at a **real-world example** of a large development team working on a complex project and how they manage their workflows with Git and GitHub.

Scenario: The development team at TechCorp is building a large e-commerce platform with several developers working on different features (e.g., product catalog, shopping cart, user authentication). The team follows a GitFlow branching model and has adopted best practices to manage their complex workflows.

Step 1: Setting Up GitFlow

The team adopts **GitFlow** to manage their branches:

- **main**: Contains stable production-ready code.
- **develop**: The integration branch where features are merged.

- ***feature/ branches****: Each feature is developed in its own branch.
- ***release/ branches****: For preparing new releases.
- ***hotfix/ branches****: For emergency fixes to the production environment.

Step 2: Automating with GitHub Actions

The team sets up **GitHub Actions** to automate testing and deployment:

- Every pull request triggers a CI workflow that runs unit tests and lints the code.
- If tests pass, the code is automatically deployed to a staging environment for further testing.

Step 3: Code Reviews and Pull Requests

- Developers create **feature branches** for each new feature (e.g., feature/product-catalog).
- Pull requests are created from these branches to **develop**.
- Each pull request is reviewed by at least one team member before it is merged. Automated tests run to verify that the code passes tests and adheres to coding standards.

Step 4: Managing Dependencies

The team uses **Git submodules** to manage a shared payment gateway library. The submodule is treated as an independent repository and is kept up to date with the latest code.

Step 5: Scaling the Team with Teams and Permissions

As the team grows, the development team is divided into sub-teams (e.g., backend, frontend, QA). **GitHub Teams** are used to manage repository access:

- The **backend team** has write access to the backend repository and read access to the frontend repository.
- The **frontend team** has write access to the frontend repository and read access to the backend repository.
- The **QA team** has access to test environments but no direct write access.

In this chapter, we covered best practices for **team collaboration** with Git and GitHub, including:

- **Branching strategies** like GitFlow and Feature Branching.
- How to **scale workflows** in large teams using GitHub Actions, submodules, and automation.
- **Real-world example** of managing a large team working on a complex project, with a clear branching strategy,

automated workflows, and efficient dependency management.

By following these practices, you can ensure that your team collaborates smoothly, even as it grows and works on more complex projects. In the next chapter, we will explore **advanced Git strategies** for managing large-scale repositories and resolving difficult issues in collaborative development.

www.ingramcontent.com/pod-product-compliance
Lightning Source LLC
LaVergne TN
LVHW051443050326
832903LV00030BD/3211

* 9 7 9 8 3 0 5 0 9 0 8 3 3 *